Fall Flavours

Photography by Julian Beveridge with the following exceptions:

Pages 11, 68, 88 — Dwayne Coon. Pages 13, 69, 95 — Keith Vaughan. Pages 16, 23, 31 — Mel Lee. Pages 26, 27, 29, 35, 39, 104 — Terry Manzo. Pages 45, 81 — Martin Caird.

Formac Publishing Company Limited acknowledges the support of the Cultural Affairs Section, Nova Scotia Department of Tourism and Culture. We acknowledge the financial support of the Government of Canada through the Book Publishing Industry Development Program (BPIDP) for our publishing activities.

This book is dedicated to our husbands, Robert and Mel, and to our families, with love, E.E. and V.L.

National Library of Canada Cataloguing in Publication Data

Elliot, Elaine, 1939-
    Fall flavours / by Elaine Elliot and Virginia Lee.

Includes index.
ISBN 0-88780-598-1

    1. Cookery. I. Lee, Virginia, 1947- II. Title.

TX714.E46 2003   641.5   C2003-902300-1

Formac Publishing Company Limited
5502 Atlantic Street
Halifax NS B3H 1G4
www.formac.ca

Printed in the People's Republic of China

Fall Flavours

ELAINE ELLIOT AND VIRGINIA LEE

Formac Publishing Company Limited
Halifax, 2003

CONTENTS

APPETIZERS & BEVERAGES 9

BREADS & BREAKFAST FOODS 21

SOUPS & SALADS 33

LUNCH 53

ENTREES   67

SIDES   87

DESSERTS   99

PRESERVES & CONDIMENTS   117

INTRODUCTION

Fall does not appear with an abrupt change of weather; instead, it creeps upon us. The hot rays of sunshine and warm breezes of summer gently give way to chilling winds, shorter days and colours that move from lush greens to bright yellows, oranges and reds through to mellow golds, rusts and browns.

As we allow the seasons to direct us, we turn from outdoor summer meals to indoor comfort food. This recipe collection will invite you to light a candle and linger over your repast, perhaps taking extra time to share the events of the day with your family or friends.

When seeking autumn-related recipes from Canadian chefs, we were inundated with suggestions for using squash and pumpkin. While there are many varieties, it appears that butternut squash, with its dense consistency, is an overall favourite. Indeed, from soups to side dishes to desserts, we found the various members of the gourd family highly respected by the cooking fraternity!

In this collection you will find vegetables combined with autumn fruit in soups and salads, innovative additions to your Thanksgiving dinner and tempting treats to end your meal. We offer suggestions for healthy breakfast fare, new ways to preserve nature's bounty for the winter months and even share recipes for our favourite autumn libations!

Fall Flavours is an independent cookbook with no

sponsorship or fees paid for inclusion. All the recipes were generously provided by professional Canadian chefs or from our own recipe collections. We would like to thank Chef Elizabeth Lee for her recipes and helpful suggestions; Catherine Briggs and her staff at Absolutely Fabulous Bed, Bath and Linens for providing props; and John Vego, Manager/ Wine Consultant at Buster's Liquors and Wines for his assistance in choosing wines to complement the luncheon and main course entrees. *Fall Flavours* offers a pictorial view of autumn fare in Canada; we are grateful to the photographers for capturing the essence of the season and to our editor, Elizabeth Eve, for her guidance.

E.E. & V.L.

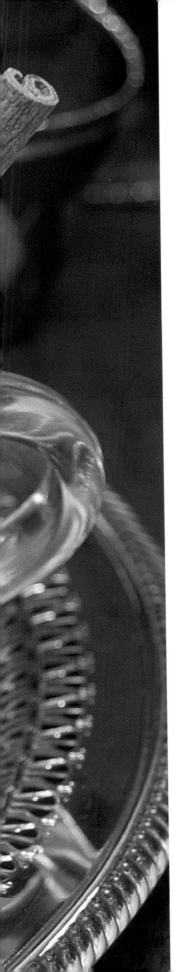

APPETIZERS & BEVERAGES

Appetizers originally evolved as a first course to ward off the initial pangs of hunger and stimulate an interest in the meal to follow. In the 21st century these small meal precursors are not limited to the main meal; instead, they are served any hour of the day and for any occasion. Serve appetizers accompanied with a beverage in the afternoon while you watch your favourite television sports event or movie, during a casual evening with friends, or at family and holiday gatherings.

In this section you will sample a wonderful variety of taste-tempting appetizers and beverages that showcase autumn's diverse bounty. This is the season for harvesting mushrooms, cranberries, apples, pears, tomatoes…the selection is endless at farm markets and fruit stands throughout the country.

Treat your guests to Chef Richard Boulier's signature Salmon Terrine from Hatfield Heritage Inn or Chef Peter Woodworth's succulent Mussels with Café de Paris Butter. When time is a factor, prepare Miniature Sweet Bell Peppers with Herb Cream Cheese or Warm Artichoke Dip.

We have included seasonal beverages that complement the changing weather. Try the Cranberry Harvest Punch during those last lovely days of Indian summer, then prepare a hot glass of Mulled Cider or Mulled Niagara Merlot with Pear when the days begin to chill.

◀ Mulled Apple Cider

MULLED APPLE CIDER

Sweet apple cider is the freshly pressed juice from apples and is available at roadside farm markets and in the refrigerated section of most grocery stores. After fermentation it becomes hard cider, and varies in alcohol content. We provide two options for your hot mulled cider — one with spirits and one without!

32 ounces/1 litre sweet apple cider

2 tablespoons brown sugar

1 teaspoon whole cloves

1 teaspoon whole allspice

2-inch/5-centimetre piece of cinnamon stick

¼ cup dark rum (optional)

Combine cider, brown sugar and spices in a large saucepan or coffee urn and heat slowly for half an hour. *Do not boil*. Discard spices and add rum, if using. Serve piping hot. *Serves 4.*

MULLED NIAGARA MERLOT WITH PEAR

HILLEBRAND'S VINEYARD CAFÉ, NIAGARA-ON-THE-LAKE, ON

The chef at Hillebrand's suggests that you "taste as you go" with this recipe — what delightful advice! The spices may be removed if you feel the flavour is too strong, add a little honey if you want a sweeter result, and if a lower alcohol content is desired, increase the cooking time.

1 cup pear juice

2-inch/5-centimetre piece fresh ginger, unpeeled and thinly sliced

1 large or 2 medium oranges

3 cups Niagara Merlot

Pinch of allspice

3 large cinnamon sticks

1 teaspoon whole cloves

3 juniper berries

Bring pear juice to room temperature and add ginger slices. Remove zest from oranges and set aside. Squeeze oranges and add zest and juice to pear juice.

Combine allspice, cinnamon sticks, cloves and juniper berries with wine in a large saucepan; bring to just under a boil and heat 40 minutes. *Do not allow the wine to boil.* Add pear juice and heat an additional 20 minutes. Strain and serve warm, adding a splash of late harvest wine if desired. *Serves 6.*

SALMON TERRINE

HATFIELD HERITAGE INN, HARTLAND, NB

Speckled with salmon, onion and parsley, this rich country-style terrine is delicious with crackers, slices of pumpernickel or baguette. The inn's signature recipe calls for smoked salmon that has been processed in the "cold-smoked" manner. Any unused terrine may be refrigerated for up to five days or frozen for up to one month.

1 pound/500 grams skinless fresh Atlantic salmon, roasted and flaked

½ pound/250 grams smoked salmon, minced

2 tablespoons fresh parsley, chopped

1 small red onion, finely diced

2 teaspoons dried tarragon

½ cup butter, softened

¾ cup mayonnaise

2 tablespoons grainy Dijon mustard

2 tablespoons lemon juice

½ teaspoon freshly ground black pepper

½ teaspoon salt

Preheat oven to 400°F. Roast fresh salmon allowing 10 minutes per inch of thickness. Cool and flake with a fork. Add smoked salmon, parsley, onion and tarragon to fresh salmon and mix to combine.

Using a separate bowl, combine butter, mayonnaise, mustard, lemon juice, pepper and salt; mix well. Slowly combine both mixtures until they are well incorporated and turn into a 1-quart/1-litre loaf pan or mould that has been lined with plastic wrap. Gently press the terrine with a spatula to remove any air bubbles.

Refrigerate until firm, approximately 4 hours. Remove from the mould and serve with crackers or bread. *Serves 8 to 10.*

MUSSELS WITH CAFÉ DE PARIS BUTTER

THE WINDSOR HOUSE OF ST. ANDREWS, ST. ANDREWS, NB

Cultivated mussels are the basis of this delightful recipe. Chef Peter Woodworth serves them warm on the half shell with anchovy-laced butter.

3 pounds/1.5 kilograms cultivated mussels, scrubbed and debearded

2 tablespoons butter

2 shallots, diced

2 cloves garlic, mashed

½ cup white wine

Anchovy Butter (recipe follows)

Scrub and debeard mussels, discarding any that have broken shells. In a large saucepan, melt the butter and sweat the shallots and garlic over medium heat until softened, about 5 minutes. Increase heat to high and stir in wine. Let the mixture reduce for 3 to 5 minutes, add mussels, cover and let steam for 5 to 6 minutes until all the shells are open. Discard any mussels that do not open.

Preheat oven to 400°F. To serve, take one half-shell off each mussel, then place the mussel in the remaining half-shell on a baking sheet. Spread a dollop of Anchovy Butter over each mussel using a small spatula. Heat in the oven 3 to 5 minutes or until the butter melts. *Serves 6.*

1 anchovy filet

1 large clove garlic

10 sprigs fresh parsley

10 capers, drained

¼ cup freshly grated Parmesan cheese

Salt and pepper to taste

2 to 3 drops Tabasco sauce

3 to 4 drops Worcestershire sauce

½ pound/250 grams butter

ANCHOVY BUTTER

Using a food processor, purée the anchovy, garlic, parsley, capers, cheese and seasonings. Cube the butter and add to mixture; process until all the ingredients are fused.

TOMATO TART

THE INN AT MANITOU, MCKELLAR, ON

Chef Bernard Ibanez selects "Roma" or Italian plum tomatoes for his Tomato Tart because they have fewer seeds and are meatier than regular salad tomatoes.

1 sheet puff pastry
½ bunch fresh basil
1 small clove garlic
½ cup extra virgin olive oil
3 to 4 large plum tomatoes, thinly sliced
Salt and pepper to taste

Preheat oven to 400°F. On a floured board, roll out puff pastry into a 10-inch/25-centimetre square and slice in half. Using a food processor, combine basil, garlic and olive oil. Arrange pastry rectangles on an ungreased baking sheet and brush with oil mixture. Fan tomato slices over top of the tarts and brush tomatoes with oil; season with salt and pepper. Bake for 18 to 20 minutes. Slice into finger portions and serve warm. *Serves 4*.

WARM ARTICHOKE DIP

A favourite of both hosts and guests, this dip can be prepared in advance and warmed just before serving. For a more robust dip, substitute the canned artichoke hearts with 2 jars of marinated artichoke hearts, drained and chopped.

1 can artichoke hearts, drained and chopped (14 ounces/397 grams)

½ cup egg-based mayonnaise

½ cup freshly grated Parmesan cheese

¼ teaspoon freshly ground pepper

1 to 2 cloves garlic, finely minced

Dash of paprika

Assorted crackers

Preheat oven to 350°F. Combine artichoke hearts, mayonnaise, Parmesan, pepper and garlic and place in an oven-safe serving dish. Sprinkle with paprika and bake until lightly browned and bubbly, about 20 minutes. Serve warm with crackers. *Makes 1½ cups.*

MINIATURE BELL PEPPERS WITH HERB CREAM CHEESE

Miniature sweet bell peppers have great flavour and wonderful visual appeal. It is almost sinful that these little hors d'oeuvres are so easy to prepare.

12 to 18 miniature red, yellow and orange sweet bell peppers

Herb Cream Cheese (recipe follows)

Halve peppers, removing seeds and membrane. Spoon or pipe with a cake decorator a small amount of Herb Cream Cheese in each pepper half. Arrange decoratively on a serving plate and serve as finger food. *Makes 24 to 36 pieces.*

8 ounces/250 grams cream cheese, softened

1 clove garlic, crushed

¼ teaspoon fresh oregano (or pinch of dried)

½ teaspoon fresh basil (or ⅛ teaspoon dried)

½ teaspoon fresh rosemary, chopped (or ⅛ teaspoon dried, crushed)

Pinch of salt

HERB CREAM CHEESE

Use this versatile cheese spread to stuff miniature sweet bell peppers or spread on crackers and crostini.

In a bowl, blend cream cheese, garlic, oregano, basil, rosemary and salt until smooth and creamy. Refrigerate, covered. *Makes 1 cup.*

CRANBERRY REFRESHERS

Cranberry juice
Chilled champagne

CRANBERRY MIMOSA

Pour equal amounts of cranberry juice and champagne into chilled flutes or other tall glasses of choice. Garnish with one of the following: mint leaves, fresh berries, sliced starfruit, orange or lime slices.

8 cups cranberry juice, chilled
2 cups grapefruit soda, chilled
2 cups soda water, chilled
ice cubes
1 lime, thinly sliced, for garnish

CRANBERRY HARVEST PUNCH

Just before serving, pour cranberry juice, grapefruit soda and soda water gently over ice cubes in a large punch bowl. Garnish with thin slices of lime. *Makes 12 cups.*

GRILLED ZUCCHINI ROLLS WITH PROSCIUTTO AND CREAM CHEESE STUFFING

The humble zucchini has never tasted so good! With its beautiful presentation, this recipe from Chef Elizabeth Lee may seem difficult, but when prepared in steps, it is really quite simple.

3 to 4 medium zucchini

¼ cup balsamic vinegar

¼ teaspoon salt

¼ teaspoon pepper

¾ cup olive oil

¼ teaspoon Dijon mustard

1 clove garlic, crushed

½ teaspoon liquid honey

6 ounces/175 grams prosciutto, thinly sliced*

Herb Cream Cheese (recipe page 16)

1½ cups mixed salad greens

1 cantaloupe, peeled, seeded and cut into 20 thin slices

Balsamic Reduction (recipe follows)

*Seasoned Italian ham, available in the deli section of supermarkets.

Cut zucchini lengthwise into 20 slices, each ⅙ inch/4 millimetres thick. In a bowl, combine vinegar, salt and pepper; add olive oil in a slow steady stream, whisking until emulsified. Dip zucchini slices in vinaigrette to coat. Arrange zucchini slices on grill preheated to medium. Reserve remaining vinaigrette. Grill zucchini, turning once, until marked and cooked through, about 6 minutes. Remove from grill and cool. To remaining vinaigrette add Dijon mustard, garlic and honey; whisk to emulsify and reserve.

To assemble, cut the prosciutto to fit the zucchini and place on top of zucchini slice. Spoon 1½ teaspoons Herb Cream Cheese on one end of the prosciutto; roll up to form a zucchini roll. Repeat the procedure, making 20 rolls in total. Lightly toss mixed greens with reserved vinaigrette.

To serve, fan 5 cantaloupe slices in a spoke-like fashion from the centre of individual serving plates. Divide salad greens and place in the centre of each plate. Place zucchini rolls between each slice of melon and drizzle Balsamic Reduction over the entire appetizer. *Serves 4.*

---

1 cup balsamic vinegar

1½ tablespoons granulated sugar

BALSAMIC REDUCTION
This all-purpose sauce can be drizzled over grilled meats, vegetables, salads — the list is only limited by your imagination. To increase the quantity, double or triple the ingredients and allow extra time for the sauce to reduce.

Combine vinegar and sugar in a small saucepan over medium-high heat, bring to a boil and reduce the liquid by three-quarters, about 15 minutes. Remove from heat and rapidly cool sauce by placing saucepan in an ice-bath. Store refrigerated; bring to room temperature before using. *Makes ¼ cup.*

SMOKED SALMON CROSTINI

Chef Elizabeth Lee serves these delicious crostini with fresh greens as a first course dish or as individual hors d'oeuvres to accompany aperitifs and cocktails. Freeze extra crostini in zip-lock plastic bags for instant appetizers when unexpected guests arrive. Remove crostini from freezer and thaw; spread with cream cheese, top with smoked salmon or proscuitto and serve immediately. For a hot appetizer, spread crostini with a savoury topping and bake in a 325°F oven until crisp, about 5 minutes.

1 baguette cut into 24 diagonal slices, ¼ inch/5 millimetres thick

Olive oil

Salt and freshly ground pepper

8 ounces/250 grams cream cheese

2 green onions, thinly sliced

1½ tablespoons capers, drained

1½ teaspoons lemon juice

Salt and pepper to taste (for cream cheese mixture)

4 ounces/125 grams smoked salmon, thinly sliced

Red onion, thinly sliced and separated into rings

Capers for garnish

Extra-virgin olive oil for garnish

Mixed greens tossed with vinaigrette of choice for garnish

Preheat oven to 325°F. Brush baguette slices with olive oil and season with salt and a generous amount of freshly ground pepper. Arrange bread on a baking sheet and bake, turning once, until crisp and lightly golden brown, about 12 minutes. Cool on rack.

In a bowl, blend together cream cheese, green onions, capers, lemon juice and salt and pepper to taste. Spread crostini with cream cheese mixture; cover with smoked salmon, top each with an onion ring and 2 to 3 capers.

To serve, arrange 4 smoked salmon crostini in a spoke-like fashion on each of 6 large plates. Place the mixed greens in the centre, where the crostini meet. In the areas between the crostini, drizzle a small amount of olive oil and sprinkle a few capers. *Serves 6*.

BREADS & BREAKFAST FOODS

As autumn approaches, breakfasts seem more important than during the warm days of summer. Fall brings routines, schedules and school — and it is important to have a nutritious meal to start the day.

In this section we have assembled a collection of recipes featuring autumn ingredients designed to tempt every palate — children will love the Pumpkin Bread liberally spread with cream cheese. Teens may fuel their day with a Breakfast Wrap, which easily adapts into a "breakfast on the run." Adults will enjoy an elegant breakfast/brunch experience when you prepare French Toast with Sautéed Apples just like they do at Gaffer's Gourmet Bistro.

Baking recipes, such as Old Fashioned Molasses Brown Bread and Spicy Cranberry Muffins, are complemented by Strawberry Jam and the Apple Butter from Inn at Spry Point.

These recipes provide a perfect start to your day, whether you are rushing off to class, heading out to work or relaxing at home on the weekend.

◀ French Toast with Sautéed Apples

FRENCH TOAST WITH SAUTÉED APPLES

GAFFER'S GOURMET BISTRO AT WHITEHALL COUNTRY INN, CLARENVILLE, NF

This combination of mouth-watering ingredients makes a late breakfast or early brunch worth the wait. The chefs at Gaffer's Gourmet Bistro prefer McIntosh apples for their flavour, juiciness and fast cooking.

1 day-old baguette, sliced on an angle, ¼ inch/5 millimetres thick

4 eggs

⅔ cup whole milk

2 tablespoons butter

1 tablespoon cinnamon

4 apples, cored, peeled and sliced into ¼-inch/5-millimetre rings

¾ to 1 cup pure maple syrup

Icing sugar for garnish

In a bowl, whisk together eggs and milk until frothy; reserve. In a large skillet over medium heat, melt butter. When butter begins to foam, dip the bread in the egg mixture and place in skillet; sprinkle with cinnamon. Fry bread, in batches, until golden brown, turn and fry other side until golden brown, remove from skillet and reserve in a warm oven.

Place the apple slices in the skillet and sauté, adding more butter if necessary, until lightly browned; turn and sauté the other side until the apples are soft and golden. Pour maple syrup over apples and simmer 1 minute.

To serve, creatively position the toast on the plates, top with the apples and syrup and sprinkle with icing sugar. *Serves 6.*

BREAKFAST WRAP

All food groups are represented in this healthy breakfast treat. Accompany the wrap with salsa or fresh fruit and you have a meal elegant enough for a sit-down breakfast or brunch; wrap it in foil and you have a travelling breakfast for those in a hurry. To make more wraps simply increase the ingredients proportionately.

4 10-inch/25-centimetre soft flour tortillas

8 eggs, lightly beaten

1 teaspoon crushed garlic

3 ounces/85 grams cheddar cheese, grated

½ cup bell pepper, finely diced

⅛ cup red onion, finely diced

3 ounces/85 grams honey ham, sliced in strips

Salt and pepper to taste

1 teaspoon vegetable oil

Cajun Cream Cheese (recipe follows)

Salsa

Parsley for garnish

Loosely wrap tortillas in a clean tea towel and place in 170°F oven until warmed, about 5 minutes. In a large bowl, combine eggs, garlic, cheddar cheese, bell pepper, onion and ham. In a large skillet, heat oil over medium heat; add egg mixture and cook, stirring gently until eggs are scrambled and set. Remove from heat and season with salt and pepper to taste.

Spread warm tortillas with Cajun Cream Cheese, top with scrambled eggs and roll up. Cut each tortilla in half on the diagonal, securing with a toothpick if necessary. Place on warmed plates; garnish with fresh parsley and serve with a dollop of salsa. *Serves 4.*

4 ounces/125 grams cream cheese, softened

½ teaspoon dried oregano

½ teaspoon Cajun seasoning

½ teaspoon salt

Freshly ground pepper to taste

CAJUN CREAM CHEESE

In a bowl, blend cream cheese, oregano, Cajun seasoning, salt and pepper until smooth and creamy. Adjust seasoning and reserve.

PUMPKIN BREAD

*Spread with softened cream cheese, pumpkin bread is a breakfast comfort food. The recipe can be doubled —
allowing one for immediate consumption and one that can be tucked away in the freezer for a busy morning treat.*

1 cup granulated sugar

1½ cups all-purpose flour

1 teaspoon baking powder

1 teaspoon soda

1 teaspoon cinnamon

½ teaspoon salt

2 eggs

½ cup vegetable oil

1 cup pumpkin purée

½ cup raisins

Preheat oven to 350°F. Sift together dry ingredients. In a bowl, whisk eggs and oil; stir in pumpkin and raisins. Add dry ingredients to pumpkin mixture, stirring until combined. Pour into a greased 9 x 5-inch/2-litre loaf pan and bake 1 hour or until a tester inserted in the centre of the loaf comes out clean. Let cool in pan for 10 minutes, remove and continue cooling on a wire rack. *Yields 1 loaf.*

OLD-FASHIONED MOLASSES BROWN BREAD

Freshly baked brown bread brings memories of mother's kitchen — a treat not often found in today's busy lifestyles. This is a simple recipe requiring a little time, but the results are marvelous.

2 tablespoons dry yeast

1 cup lukewarm water

3 cups hot water

1 tablespoon salt

3 tablespoons shortening

1 cup molasses

2 cups rolled oats

8 cups all-purpose flour

Sprinkle dry yeast over lukewarm water and stir to dissolve. Let stand 10 minutes or until mixture doubles in size. In a large bowl, place hot water, salt, shortening, molasses and rolled oats. Beat mixture and allow to cool. Stir in the yeast mixture and add flour, a cupful at a time, mixing until well incorporated. Turn onto a floured board and knead until smooth, about 7 to 10 minutes. Shape into a ball and place in a lightly greased bowl, turning once to grease surface. Cover and let rise in a warm, draft-free place until it doubles in volume, about 1 hour.

Punch down dough, divide in half and shape into two loaves. Place in 2 greased 9 x 5-inch/2-litre loaf pans. Cover and let rise 1 hour.

Preheat oven to 350°F. Bake for 1 hour or until golden brown. Remove from pans and cool on wire racks. *Yields 2 loaves.*

BUTTERMILK BISCUITS

CHIVES CANADIAN BISTRO, HALIFAX, NS

Sweet or savoury, the choice is yours! At Chives Canadian Bistro, the chefs serve their warm biscuits as a savoury appetizer base for foie gras and chutney. We have included this versatile recipe because the biscuits are equally delicious served as a bread accompaniment or, without the chives, as the base for a sweet dessert.

2 cups all-purpose flour

1 tablespoon baking powder

2 teaspoons sugar

¼ teaspoon salt

½ cup butter

1 egg

1 cup buttermilk

¼ cup chopped chives

Preheat oven to 400°F. In a mixing bowl, combine flour, baking powder, sugar and salt. Using a pastry blender, cut in butter until mixture resembles coarse crumbs. Whisk together the egg and buttermilk, mix in the chives and add to dry mixture, stirring lightly with a fork to make a soft dough. Turn out onto a floured board and gently knead 2 or 3 times. Form each biscuit by dropping a tablespoon of dough onto a lightly greased baking sheet and bake until golden, approximately 15 minutes. For large biscuits, cut with a 2-inch/5-centimetre cutter and bake 30 to 35 minutes. *Yields 36 tiny or 10 large biscuits.*

SPICY CRANBERRY MUFFINS

WESTOVER INN, ST. MARYS, ON

Brimming with cranberries, these muffins are best served warm. Pastry chef Ruth Moxley of Westover Inn says you may use either fresh or frozen cranberries.

2½ cups all-purpose flour

½ cup sugar

½ cup brown sugar

2 teaspoons baking powder

½ teaspoon baking soda

½ teaspoon salt

2 teaspoons cinnamon

¼ teaspoon nutmeg

2 eggs, beaten

⅔ cup vegetable oil

¾ cup buttermilk

½ teaspoon vanilla

1 cup cranberries

Preheat oven to 400°F. In a large bowl, combine flour, sugars, baking powder, soda, salt, cinnamon and nutmeg. In a separate bowl, whisk together the eggs, oil, buttermilk and vanilla. Stir wet mixture into dry ingredients, add cranberries and stir just until combined. Fill paper-lined muffin tins three-quarters full and bake 25 minutes or until muffins are golden brown and spring back when touched. *Yields 12 to 16 muffins.*

JOHNNY CAKE

There are probably as many renditions of Johnny Cake as there are cookbooks — ranging from flat cornmeal pancakes to leavened breads, served warm in squares. This is the Johnny Cake of our childhood; a wonderful addition to suppers of homemade soups or baked beans.

2 cups all-purpose flour

5 teaspoons baking powder

½ teaspoon baking soda

½ teaspoon salt

1 cup cornmeal

½ cup granulated sugar

2 eggs, beaten

½ cup molasses

1½ cups milk

½ cup melted butter

Preheat oven to 350°F. Combine flour, baking powder, baking soda, salt, cornmeal and sugar. In a separate bowl, combine eggs, molasses, milk and melted butter. Add dry ingredients to wet ingredients, a little at a time, stirring to combine. Pour into a greased, deep 9 x 12-inch/3-litre baking pan and bake 50 to 55 minutes or until a toothpick inserted in the centre comes out clean. *Serve warm.*

STRAWBERRY JAM

WESTOVER INN, ST. MARYS, ON

At Westover Inn, the chefs prepare jams and condiments for use year-round in their dining rooms, and strawberry jam is a perennial favourite. Use fresh or frozen berries in this recipe. If using fresh fruit, wash, hull and then crush the berries. If using frozen berries, allow them to thaw completely in a container deep enough to hold all of the juice and then crush the berries with the juice.

4 cups crushed strawberries

¼ cup lemon juice

7 cups granulated sugar

1 envelope liquid fruit pectin

Wash and sterilize jars and prepare lids as manufacturer directs. Place berries and lemon juice in a large pot, being careful to fill container no more than half full; set over high heat and bring to a boil, stirring every few minutes. Add sugar and stir well, bring back to a boil and boil hard for 1 minute. Remove from heat and stir in the liquid fruit pectin. Continue stirring for 6 minutes, stopping to skim off the foam 2 or 3 times. Pour into hot sterilized jars and cover with prepared lids and rims. Allow to cool and check the seal by ensuring the lids are curved down slightly. Refrigerate after opening. *Yields 8 cups of jam.*

RASPBERRY JAM WITH COINTREAU

Cointreau or any orange liqueur adds a subtle flavour to this sweet preserve. For those who prefer a jam with fewer seeds, simply remove some seeds by straining half the purée before cooking.

4 cups raspberries

¼ cup lemon juice

6½ cups granulated sugar

1 envelope liquid fruit pectin

2 tablespoons Cointreau liqueur

Wash and sterilize jars and prepare lids as manufacturer directs. Crush berries, a layer at a time, and press half the mixture through a sieve to remove seeds, if desired. Place in a large preserving kettle, add lemon juice and sugar, stirring until sugar is dissolved. Place over high heat and bring to a full rolling boil, stirring constantly. Boil hard for 1 minute. Remove from heat and immediately stir in the liquid fruit pectin. Stir and skim for 5 minutes. Stir in liqueur. Pour quickly into hot sterilized jars and cover with prepared lids and rims. Allow to cool and check the seal by ensuring the lids are curved down slightly. Store in a cool cupboard for up to 6 months. *Yields 8 cups of jam*.

APPLE BUTTER

THE INN AT SPRY POINT, SPRY POINT, PEI

Those who love the flavour of spicy apples will appreciate this recipe for old-fashioned apple preserve. Serve the butter warm or cold on toast, muffins and breads. Choose apple varieties that appeal to your personal taste buds, as the end flavour depends upon the type of apple you use.

9 cooking apples, peeled, cored and quartered

1 cup apple cider (or apple juice)

1½ cups granulated sugar

½ cup brown sugar

1½ teaspoons cinnamon

¼ teaspoon allspice

Dash of nutmeg

2 tablespoons cider vinegar

In a large heavy-bottomed saucepan over medium heat, bring apples and apple cider to a boil. Cover saucepan, reduce heat to simmer and cook, stirring occasionally, until apples are soft, about 25 to 30 minutes (the time will vary according to the variety of apple used).

In a food processor, purée the apples until smooth. Return the mixture to saucepan and add remaining ingredients. Cook over low heat, stirring frequently, until mixture becomes thick, about 30 minutes. Spoon into plastic containers, cover and freeze, or pour into preserving jars, seal and process in a hot-water bath for 10 minutes. *Makes 5 cups.*

SOUPS & SALADS

As the chill of autumn approaches, we look forward to warm, substantial soups that take advantage of harvest vegetables. We asked chefs across the country to share their special autumn recipes to create a collection that represents the season. Mature fall fruits and vegetables are the basis for these tempting dishes, which are sprinkled generously with each chef's personal style.

Soup and salad may go hand-in-hand at lunchtime and follow one another in the evening. The Salad of Organic Field Greens with Orange Shallot Vinaigrette from Chives Canadian Bistro is a simple-to-prepare salad enhanced by fresh fall apples and smoked nuts. Late season field tomatoes are at their sweetest when picked just before the first frost and Wellington Court's version of Field Tomato Soup with Goat Cheese Cream and Chive Oil bursts with robust tomato flavour and makes an elegant presentation. Numerous chefs shared special recipes for squash soups and Butternut Soup with Shrimp and Cinnamon Croutons from Little Shemogue Country Inn is one of our favourites.

Soups and salads are a wonderful addition to your diet. Note that while many of the soups call for heavy cream in the list of ingredients, in testing we found that lighter creams or milk give good results.

◀ Field Tomato Soup with Goat Cheese and Chive Oil

CREAMY LEEK AND SPINACH SOUP

SEAWIND LANDING COUNTRY INN, CHARLOS COVE, NS

Early autumn is the ideal harvest time for leeks. Although they are closely related to both garlic and onions, their subtle flavour is much milder. Choose leeks with bright green leaves and an unblemished white portion, and rinse carefully because soil may be embedded between the leafy layers.

1½ pounds/750 grams leeks, white and pale green parts only, about 3 cups

6 tablespoons butter, divided

¼ cup dry white wine

Pinch of sugar

3½ cups chicken stock

1-pound/500-gram package fresh spinach, rinsed and stemmed

1 cup coarsely chopped flat-leaf parsley

½ cup heavy cream (35% mf)

Salt and pepper to taste

Using only the white and pale green parts, carefully wash and slice the leeks. Melt 3 tablespoons butter in a heavy stockpot and sauté leeks until soft but not coloured, approximately 8 minutes. Add wine and sugar and simmer, stirring occasionally, until all liquid has evaporated, about 4 minutes. Stir in stock. Set aside 2 cups of prepared spinach leaves and stir remainder into stock. Cook for 2 minutes until spinach wilts. Mix in parsley, bring to a boil, then reduce heat and simmer, covered, for 10 minutes. In a food processor, purée soup with the two reserved cups of spinach until smooth.

To serve, return soup to stock pot and bring to a simmer. Add cream and season with salt and pepper. Whisk in 3 tablespoons butter. *Serves 4 to 6.*

VEGETABLE CHOWDER

WESTOVER INN, ST. MARYS, ON

The chef comments that with the addition of seafood, this flavourful chowder can be served as a main course. Accompany the soup with crusty bread and wedges of aged cheddar cheese.

3 cups chicken stock

2 cups whole milk (3½% mf)

½ cup white wine

2 tablespoons butter

2 tablespoons olive oil

1 medium onion, diced

1 medium leek, diced (white part only)

2 carrots, diced

2 celery stalks, diced

2 medium potatoes, ½-inch/1-centimetre dice

2 cloves garlic, minced

½ teaspoon saffron

3 tablespoons all-purpose flour

1½ cups corn kernels

1 small bay leaf

½ cup heavy cream (35% mf)

2 tablespoons fresh dill, chopped

Salt to taste

Dill sprigs for garnish

In a saucepan, bring stock, milk and wine to boil, stirring constantly. Reduce heat and simmer, stirring occasionally, for 10 minutes; keep hot.

In a large skillet, heat butter and oil over medium heat; sauté onion, leek, carrots, celery, potatoes, garlic and saffron. Gradually stir in flour just until absorbed by butter and oil. Increase heat to high; add hot stock mixture, stirring constantly, until thickened.

Reduce heat and add corn, bay leaf, cream and dill; simmer until vegetables are al dente. Taste and adjust seasoning with salt; remove the bay leaf. Serve in soup bowls garnished with a sprig of dill. *Serves 4 to 6.*

FIELD TOMATO SOUP WITH GOAT CHEESE CREAM AND CHIVE OIL

WELLINGTON COURT RESTAURANT, ST. CATHARINES, ON

This is a great recipe to prepare when you have those large, sweet late-in-the-season tomatoes hanging on the vine. At Wellington Court the Chive Oil is prepared with truffle oil. Extra-virgin olive oil will provide the same lovely green colour, and though the taste may not be quite as exotic, it is nevertheless very good.

4 tablespoons olive oil

3 medium shallots, minced (or ½ cup finely chopped onion)

2 pounds/1 kilogram large ripe field tomatoes, seeded and chopped

Pinch of granulated sugar

2 cups chicken or vegetable stock

Salt and pepper

2 tablespoons chèvre (goat's-milk cheese)

1 tablespoon water

Chive Oil (recipe follows)

Heat olive oil in a saucepan over medium heat; add shallots and cook for 1 minute. Add tomatoes, granulated sugar and stock, bring to a boil; reduce heat and simmer 20 minutes. In a food processor, purée soup in batches until smooth. Return soup to saucepan over low heat and season with salt and pepper to taste.

In a food processor, process chèvre until softened; slowly add water, one teaspoon at a time, until the cheese is of pouring consistency. The amount of water used will depend on the type of chèvre. Adjust seasoning with salt and pepper.

To serve, ladle soup in 4 shallow soup bowls. Creatively drizzle chèvre sauce and Chive Oil on top of soup. *Serves 4.*

---

6 tablespoons chives, chopped

6 tablespoons extra-virgin olive oil (or truffle oil)

CHIVE OIL

This bright green oil can be used to season or garnish a variety of soups, salads and vegetables.

In a food processor, process chives until minced; slowly add olive oil in a steady stream and process until puréed. Pass mixture through a fine-mesh sieve; discard chive mulch and reserve oil. *Makes ⅓ cup of oil.*

CREAM OF CHANTERELLE SOUP

CHANTERELLE COUNTRY INN, NORTH RIVER, ST. ANNS BAY, NS

If chanterelles are unavailable, substitute other mushrooms such as shiitake, cremini or oyster to achieve an earthy flavour. In testing, we used blend cream, but for a creamier soup use table or heavy cream.

2 to 3 tablespoons olive oil

1 medium onion, chopped

1 shallot, finely chopped

2 cloves garlic, finely diced

½ cup celery, diced

¼ cup shredded carrot

½ pound chanterelles, coarsely chopped

2 cups chicken stock

1 cup heavy cream (35% mf)

Salt and pepper to taste

Snipped chervil or parsley for garnish

Sauté onion, shallot and garlic in olive oil until soft and lightly golden. Stir in celery and carrot and cook 1 minute. Add mushrooms and cook 2 minutes, stirring frequently. Add stock and simmer, covered, 10 minutes. In a food processor, pulse soup until slightly chunky. Return soup to saucepan, add cream and reheat, being careful not to boil. Adjust seasonings with salt and pepper and garnish with chervil.
Serves 4.

APPLE AND PARSNIP SOUP

AUBERGE LE VIEUX PRESBYTÈRE, BOUCTOUCHE, NB

Chase away the chills of autumn with this warm soup! Fresh apples and sweet parsnips are simmered in the stock, creating a delightful blend of flavours.

1 tablespoon butter

1 medium onion, chopped

1 small stalk of celery, chopped

4 cups chicken stock

1 pound parsnips, peeled and chopped

2 medium apples, peeled and chopped

⅓ cup light cream (18% mf)

Salt and pepper to taste

Chopped parsley for garnish

In a large saucepan, melt butter over medium heat; cook onion and celery for 3 to 5 minutes or until softened. Add stock and parsnips; cover and bring to a boil. Reduce heat to medium-low and simmer 15 minutes or until parsnips are tender. Add apples; simmer 15 minutes longer or until apples are tender. In a blender, purée mixture in batches until smooth. Return soup to saucepan and stir in cream. Season with salt and pepper and bring to serving temperature, being careful not to boil. Garnish bowls with chopped parsley. *Serves 4 to 6*.

SWEET POTATO AND ROASTED RED PEPPER SOUP

WESTOVER INN, ST. MARYS, ON

Roasting red peppers releases their pungent flavour and is well worth the few minutes spent on preparation. This is a full-bodied soup, thickened by the sweet potato purée, and ideal for those concerned with fat content in their diet.

2 sweet red peppers

1½ pounds/750 grams sweet potatoes

½ medium onion

1½ teaspoons butter

1½ teaspoons olive oil

½ teaspoon salt

¼ teaspoon pepper

4 cups chicken stock

Sour cream or chives for garnish

Preheat oven to 400°F. Place peppers on a cookie sheet and roast until skin is brown and blistered, approximately 30 minutes. Remove peppers, place in a bowl and cover with plastic wrap. Refrigerate until completely cool.

Once peppers are cool, peel off skin and remove seeds. Set flesh aside and discard skin and seeds.

Peel sweet potatoes and cut into small pieces. Peel onion and chop. In a large pot over medium heat, sauté onion with oil and butter until soft, add potatoes and cook for about 2 to 3 minutes. Season with salt and pepper and add red peppers and stock. Simmer until potatoes are very soft; purée mixture in batches in a blender until soup is smooth and velvety. Serve hot, garnished with a dollop of sour cream or snipped chives. *Serves 6.*

ROASTED ONION AND GARLIC SOUP WITH BRIE CROUTONS AND CARAMELIZED ONION (MINESTRA DI CIPOLLE E AGLIO ARROSTO)

LA PERLA, DARTMOUTH, NS

You will love the subtle sweet onion and roasted garlic flavour that permeates this mild soup. Spanish and red Italian are the most common sweet onions available, but look for other seasonal varieties such as American Vidalia, Walla Walla and Texas Sweet, or South American Oso Sweet and Mayan onions.

Refrigerate onions for 30 minutes before slicing to reduce tears.

2 pounds/1 kilogram Spanish onions, thinly sliced, plus another Spanish onion, thinly sliced

4 heads garlic, broken into cloves and peeled

¼ cup olive oil

¾ cup dry white wine

7 cups rich chicken stock

Salt and pepper to taste

1 tablespoon butter

¼ cup superfine sugar

6 slices Brie

6 slices rustic bread

Preheat oven to 375°F. Spread first measure of onions and garlic in a large roasting pan, drizzle with olive oil and bake in oven for 1 to 1½ hours, stirring occasionally, until onions and garlic are a nice golden colour. Deglaze roasting pan with wine, stirring to release flavourful caramelized residue. Transfer mixture to a large pot and add chicken stock. Bring soup to a gentle simmer and cook 20 minutes, stirring occasionally.

In a food processor or blender, purée soup in batches to desired consistency. If you want very smooth soup, pass the purée through a fine-mesh strainer. Return soup to pot, adjust seasoning with salt and pepper and keep warm.

Melt butter in a skillet over medium heat; add second measure of onions, stirring constantly until onions begin to soften. Add sugar; reduce heat to low and cook, stirring frequently, until onions are caramelized and golden. Place cheese slices on bread slices and broil until cheese is melted and bread crisps.

To serve, ladle the soup into large bowls, place a cheese crouton in the centre and top with caramelized onions. *Serves 6.*

ROASTED YAM AND PEAR SOUP

CELLAR DOOR BISTRO AT SUMAC RIDGE ESTATE WINERY, SUMMERLAND, BC

The deep aroma of this recipe is achieved by roasting the yam cubes. The chef advises that the addition of cream is optional, and in testing we found the soup very creamy in texture and full of zest without the cream.

1 pound/500 grams yams (or sweet potatoes), peeled and cut into 1-inch/2.5-centimetre cubes

3 tablespoons vegetable oil

1½ tablespoons brown sugar

1 medium onion, diced

6 fresh sage leaves, minced

3 tablespoons butter

2 Bartlett pears, peeled, seeded and chopped

4 cups chicken or vegetable stock

Salt and pepper to taste

½ cup heavy (35% mf) cream (optional)

Preheat oven to 350°F. Toss yam cubes with oil and brown sugar and spread in a single layer on a baking sheet. Roast in oven for 30 minutes or until soft and slightly caramelized.

In a large saucepan, sauté onion and sage in butter for 5 minutes, add yams, pears and stock. Bring to a boil, reduce heat and simmer 15 minutes. Purée soup, return to saucepan and season to taste with salt and pepper. Stir in cream, if desired. *Serves 4.*

BUTTERNUT SOUP WITH SHRIMP AND CINNAMON CROUTONS

LITTLE SHEMOGUE COUNTRY INN, PORT ELGIN, NB

With its pungently aromatic flavour, this soup is like a good movie that you keep talking about long after you have left the theatre. It is so satisfying that you will want to experience it again and again.

3 tablespoons butter

1 large onion, chopped

2 cloves garlic, minced

2 tablespoons fresh ginger, minced

1½ tablespoons curry powder

½ tablespoon each salt and pepper

Pinch of paprika

Pinch of chili powder

½ cup celery, chopped

½ cup red pepper, diced

5 cups butternut squash, peeled and cubed

1 large potato, peeled and diced

4 cups chicken stock

Juice of 1 orange

2 tablespoons tomato paste

4 tablespoons coconut milk

1 cup heavy cream (35% mf)

Garlic Shrimp (recipe follows)

Cinnamon Croutons (recipe follows)

In a large saucepan over medium heat, melt butter; add onion, garlic, ginger, curry powder, salt and pepper, paprika and chili. Cook, stirring frequently, for 3 minutes until softened. Add celery and red pepper and cook an additional 3 minutes. Add squash and potato and stir until well coated. Add chicken stock, orange juice and tomato paste; bring to a boil, cover and reduce heat to simmer. Cook until vegetables are very tender, about 20 minutes.

In a blender or food processor, purée soup in batches until smooth; return to saucepan. Add coconut milk and cream to purée, and heat until steaming, being careful not to boil.

To serve, ladle the soup into bowls, place a couple of shrimp in the centre of each bowl and top with croutons. *Serves 6*.

---

1 tablespoon olive oil

12 large raw shrimp, peeled

2 cloves garlic, minced

Pinch of salt

1 tablespoon fresh parsley, minced

GARLIC SHRIMP

Heat olive oil in a skillet over medium heat, add shrimp and stir until they turn pink. Add garlic, salt and parsley; cook and stir 1 minute.

---

2 tablespoons butter

2 slices good quality white bread, crusts removed, and cut into large cubes

½ teaspoon cinnamon (or to taste)

CINNAMON CROUTONS

In a skillet, heat butter over medium-high heat; add croutons and stir until they brown. Add cinnamon, stirring to coat.

CELERY ROOT SOUP WITH OYSTER FRITTERS

INN AT BAY FORTUNE, BAY FORTUNE, PEI

Celery root, or celeriac, tastes like a cross between celery and parsley and is available in the fall and winter. To prevent the vegetable from discolouring, peel and soak briefly in water to which a small amount of lemon juice or vinegar has been added.

2 tablespoons butter

½ pound/250 grams celery root, peeled, soaked and coarsely chopped

1 large sweet onion, chopped

2 cloves garlic, crushed

2 bay leaves

1 bouquet garni (recipe follows)

6 cups chicken stock

Salt and white pepper to taste

Extra-virgin olive oil for garnish

Oyster Fritters (recipe follows)

In a large heavy-bottomed saucepan over low heat, melt butter and sweat celery root and onion until onion is softened, about 6 to 8 minutes. Add garlic and bay leaves and cook an additional 2 minutes. Add bouquet garni and chicken stock to saucepan and bring to boil, reduce heat to low, cover and simmer 45 minutes.

Remove bouquet garni and bay leaves. In a blender, purée soup in batches until smooth. Strain soup purée through a fine-mesh strainer; return to saucepan and adjust seasoning with salt and white pepper.

To serve, ladle soup into soup bowls and garnish with drops of extra-virgin olive oil; accompany with Oyster Fritters. *Serves 6.*

1 leek, green top only, chopped

1 small bunch flat-leaf parsley

1 bunch fresh thyme

¼ teaspoon white peppercorns

1 bay leaf

BOUQUET GARNI

Combine all ingredients in a cheesecloth bag.

Vegetable oil for shallow frying

1 cup soda water

1 teaspoon baking powder

Pinch of salt and pepper

½ to ¾ cup all-purpose flour

18 fresh oysters

OYSTER FRITTERS

At Inn at Bay Fortune, local Colville Bay oysters are used in this recipe.

In a skillet, add vegetable oil to a depth of ¼ inch/5 millimetres and heat to 365°F. In a bowl, stir together soda water, baking powder and a pinch of salt and pepper. Whisk in enough flour to form a light batter.

Dip oysters in the batter. Fry oysters, a few at a time, turning as necessary to achieve a nice golden colour. Remove and drain briefly on paper towels to absorb extra fat. Keep warm until serving. *Makes 18 fritters*.

GOLDEN HARVEST SOUP

GABRIEAU'S BISTRO, ANTIGONISH, NS

The old adage "use what you have on hand" applies to owner/chef Mark Gabrieau as he transforms an abundant supply of fresh seasonal vegetables into this hearty soup.

⅓ cup butter

1 medium onion, diced

2 stalks celery, diced

1 large leek, white part only, diced

2 large carrots, diced

½ butternut squash, diced

1 clove garlic, minced

1 teaspoon fresh ginger, minced or ½ teaspoon dried

1 bay leaf

¼ teaspoon dried thyme

½ teaspoon nutmeg

1 tablespoon brown sugar

3 tablespoons white wine

5 cups chicken stock

½ to 1 cup heavy cream (35% mf) or blend cream (10% mf)

Salt and pepper to taste

Melt butter over medium heat and sauté onion, celery, leek, carrots, squash, garlic and ginger until vegetables soften and turn golden brown. Add bay leaf, thyme, nutmeg, brown sugar, wine and stock. Cover, reduce heat and simmer for approximately 35 minutes. Remove from heat and discard bay leaf. In a blender, purée soup in batches until smooth. Adjust consistency with cream and season to taste with salt and pepper. Reheat to serving temperature, being careful not to boil. *Serves 4 to 6.*

JERUSALEM ARTICHOKE SOUP

CAFÉ BRIO, VICTORIA, BC

Jerusalem artichokes (or sunchokes) are neither artichokes nor found in Jerusalem! Indeed, they are the tuberous root of a plant related to the sunflower, and are a crop harvested in late autumn. At Cafe Brio the chef serves his soup with a swirl of truffle oil and crostini or croutons.

1 medium yellow onion, diced

¼ cup butter

1 cup white wine

2 pounds/1 kilogram Jerusalem artichokes, peeled and sliced

1 medium Yukon gold potato, peeled and sliced

4 cups chicken stock

½ bunch fresh thyme

½ cup heavy cream (35% mf)

Salt and pepper to taste

Truffle oil, arugula oil, crostini or croutons for garnish (optional)

Sweat onions in butter over low heat until translucent; stir in wine and reduce volume by half. Add Jerusalem artichokes, potato, stock and thyme; bring to a boil, reduce heat and simmer until vegetables are soft. Remove from heat and discard thyme. In a blender, purée soup in batches until smooth. Add cream, season with salt and pepper and return to serving temperature, being careful not to boil. Garnish, if desired, with a swirl of oil and croutons. *Serves 4 to 6.*

SPINACH SALAD

BEILD HOUSE, COLLINGWOOD, ON

This salad adapts well to a variety of fruits such as mandarin oranges, strawberries, kiwis, grapefruit, mangoes or papaya.

Fresh spinach greens to serve 6

Sweet Poppyseed Dressing (recipe follows)

1 cup sliced fruit

½ small red onion, thinly sliced in rings

Spicy Almonds (recipe follows)

Rinse and dry spinach, removing tough stems. Tear spinach into bite-size pieces and combine in a large salad bowl. Drizzle with Sweet Poppyseed Dressing and toss; add fruit and onion rings and lightly toss again. Divide between 6 large plates and top with Spicy Almonds. *Serves 6.*

¼ cup raspberry vinegar

3 tablespoons granulated sugar

1 tablespoon poppyseeds

¼ teaspoon paprika

2 teaspoons onion, minced

¼ teaspoon Worcestershire sauce

½ cup vegetable oil

SWEET POPPYSEED DRESSING

In a small bowl, stir the vinegar and sugar together; microwave on high for 30 seconds to break down the sugar crystals. In a blender, process vinegar and sugar, poppyseeds, paprika, onion and Worcestershire sauce for 30 seconds. With blender running, add vegetable oil in a slow steady stream, blending until emulsified. *Makes 1 cup.*

¼ cup granulated sugar

2 teaspoons water

1 teaspoon butter

1 teaspoon cinnamon

½ teaspoon ground ginger

½ teaspoon ground nutmeg

½ cup sliced almonds

SPICY ALMONDS

These candied almonds may also be used as a topping for ice cream or other desserts.

In a skillet over medium heat, combine the sugar, water, butter and spices; stir to dissolve. Add the almonds and continue cooking, stirring constantly until the almonds are coated and slightly caramelized, about 5 minutes. Turn out onto greased foil; break up when cool and store in a covered container. *Makes 1 cup.*

SALAD OF ORGANIC FIELD GREENS WITH ORANGE SHALLOT VINAIGRETTE

CHIVES CANADIAN BISTRO, HALIFAX, NS

To provide contrast, the chef at Chives suggests a mix of mild and bitter salad greens, such as arugula, oak leaf, mâche and radicchio. He tops his salad with a drizzle of vinaigrette bursting with the flavour of shallots.

Organic field greens to serve 4

⅔ cup crumbled Danish Blue cheese

½ cup smoked almonds

1 Granny Smith apple, in julienne strips

Orange Shallot Vinaigrette (recipe follows)

Clean greens and divide between four chilled plates. Sprinkle greens with cheese, smoked almonds and apple strips; drizzle with Orange Shallot Vinaigrette. *Serves 4.*

1 cup freshly squeezed orange juice

Zest of one orange, minced

2 small shallots, finely minced

1 tablespoon honey vinegar or 2 teaspoons white vinegar and 1 teaspoon liquid honey

¾ cup light olive oil

Salt and pepper

1 teaspoon sugar (optional)

ORANGE SHALLOT VINAIGRETTE

Over medium-high heat, reduce the orange juice to ¼ cup. Add zest, shallots and honey vinegar to hot juice. Place mixture in a blender and with motor running, add olive oil in a slow steady stream until emulsified. Adjust seasoning with salt and pepper, and sugar, if desired; refrigerate. *Makes 1 cup.*

ROMAINE SALAD WITH APPLE MAPLE DRESSING

THE BRIARS INN AND COUNTRY CLUB, JACKSON'S POINT, ON

Executive Chef Trevor Ledlie of The Briars Inn advises that he occasionally substitutes pears for the apples in this delicious dressing. Whichever fruit you choose, we are sure you will find the dressing delightful.

1 large head romaine lettuce

½ pint cherry tomatoes, halved

½ English-style cucumber, sliced

2 to 3 mushrooms, thinly sliced

Apple Maple Dressing (recipe follows)

Rinse, dry and tear romaine into bite-size pieces and divide between 4 chilled salad plates. Top with cherry tomato halves, cucumber and mushroom slices; drizzle with Apple Maple Dressing. *Serves 4.*

½ apple, cored, peeled and chopped

3 tablespoons apple juice

½ tablespoon mayonnaise

½ tablespoon pure maple syrup

¼ cup white wine vinegar

½ cup olive oil

¼ teaspoon chopped cilantro

Salt and pepper to taste

APPLE MAPLE DRESSING

Combine all ingredients in a high-speed blender and purée until smooth. Store any unused dressing refrigerated in a jar up to 1 week. *Makes 1 cup.*

LUNCH

Autumn is a time of beginnings and endings. Students return to class, meetings resume and we generally find time to catch up on delayed projects, while the daylight hours shorten and the warm breezes of summer fade into memory. What better season to invite a new friend or an old acquaintance to a spectacular lunch?

These lunch selections include a diverse collection of tantalizing fall recipes such as Rotini with Wild Fungi Sauce, Mussels in Love and Harvest Vegetable Polenta Torte, the creation of the chef at Waverley, Nova Scotia's Inn on the Lake. These recipes elevate comfort food to the height of gourmet fare!

Be sure to sample Rosemary Seared Scallops with Dried Apple Butter from the Cellar Door Bistro in Summerland, BC, or try Halifax's Opa Taverna's Spanakopita. Increase the quantities and many of the luncheon recipes would make excellent entrees.

Fall is the season when the vegetable markets are laden with produce, so be adventuresome, then take the time to enjoy your creations.

◀ Spanakopita

SPANAKOPITA

OPA GREEK TAVERNA, HALIFAX, NS

At Opa Greek Taverna, the chef serves his spanakopita in triangles. Phyllo pastry is found in the freezer section of larger grocery stores and should be thawed as the package directs.

½ cup extra-virgin olive oil, divided

½ sweet onion, finely diced

½ cup green onion, chopped

½ leek, washed and finely diced, white part only

1 pound fresh spinach, cleaned, stems removed and chopped

¼ cup parsley, chopped

¼ cup fresh dill, chopped

1 egg, beaten

1 cup feta cheese, crumbled

Pinch of nutmeg

Salt and pepper to taste

12 to 16 sheets phyllo pastry

Heat 3 tablespoons of the olive oil in a large saucepan over medium-low heat and sauté the onion, green onions and leek until soft. Stir in spinach and cook until wilted. Place in a large bowl and add parsley, dill, egg, cheese and nutmeg. Season with salt and pepper and mix well to combine.

Preheat oven to 375°F. Place a sheet of phyllo pastry on a work surface and brush lightly with remaining olive oil. Top with 3 more sheets of pastry, brushing each with oil, then cut into 4 equal rectangles. Spoon 2 tablespoons of spinach mixture on each rectangle; fold into triangle shapes and brush the tops with olive oil. Repeat process with remaining phyllo sheets, making 12 to 16 triangles in all. Bake on a lightly greased baking sheet until golden brown, approximately 15 to 20 minutes. Serve warm. *Serves 6.*

Wine suggestion: Italian Pinot Grigio

MUSSELS IN LOVE

CASTLE ROCK COUNTRY INN, INGONISH FERRY, NS

While farm-raised mussels are available year-round, Chef Jason Bailey of Castle Rock Country Inn tells us that they are plumpest in the fall. We caution that the peppers suggested are extremely hot on the skin, so handle with care. Increase the quantities in this recipe and you have a wonderful dinner entree.

3 pounds/1.5 kilograms fresh mussels

1½ tablespoons olive oil

1½ tablespoons butter

1½ tablespoons shallots, minced

½ to 1 teaspoon Habanero chili pepper, minced (or substitute Scotch bonnet or jalapeno)

1½ teaspoons rosemary

½ teaspoon black pepper

2 cloves garlic, minced

1¼ cups dry white wine

1 cup grated Monterey Jack cheese

1 tablespoon all-purpose flour

2 cups heavy cream (35% mf)

8 to 10 ounces/250 to 300 grams angel hair pasta, linguine or fettuccine, cooked al dente

Chopped cilantro and rosemary sprigs for garnish

Scrub and debeard mussels, discarding any that have broken shells. Melt the oil and butter in a large saucepan over medium-low heat and sauté shallots, hot peppers, rosemary and black pepper for 3 minutes. Add garlic and mussels and sauté another 3 minutes, stirring occasionally to coat. Add wine, raise heat to medium high, cover saucepan and steam mussels until open, approximately 5 minutes. Remove mussels from pot, discarding any that did not open. Set aside and keep warm, reserving the cooking broth.

Toss Monterey Jack cheese with flour and combine with mussel broth in a saucepan. Bring to a boil, reduce heat and cook, stirring constantly, until thickened, about 5 minutes. Stir in cream and bring back to serving temperature, being careful not to boil.

Divide pasta between four plates and arrange mussels in their shells decoratively on top of the pasta. Drizzle the sauce over the mussels and garnish with freshly chopped cilantro and a sprig of fresh rosemary. *Serves 4.*

Wine suggestion: Dry Riesling

ROSEMARY SEARED SCALLOPS WITH DRIED APPLE BUTTER

CELLAR DOOR BISTRO AT SUMAC RIDGE ESTATE WINERY, SUMMERLAND, BC

Choose your scallops carefully, making sure they have a fresh sweet smell and have not been artificially plumped with water to increase their weight.

2 shallots, finely sliced

3 teaspoons olive oil, divided

1 sprig of rosemary, stem removed

Freshly ground black pepper to taste

⅔ cup fish stock

12 to 18 dried apple rings (quantity depends on size of rings)

12 large sea scallops

½ cup white wine

6 tablespoons butter, cubed and slightly softened

Salt to taste

Rosemary sprigs for garnish

In a saucepan over low heat, sweat shallots in 1 teaspoon olive oil until soft, about 8 minutes; add rosemary and pepper and cook 1 additional minute. Add the fish stock and bring to a boil; reduce heat to simmer and cook 3 minutes. In a bowl, combine the shallot mixture and apple rings. Let apples rehydrate until cool. This may be done several hours in advance.

Rinse scallops, pat dry and lightly brush with remaining olive oil. Heat a heavy-based skillet to very hot; sear scallops to colour both sides, being careful not to overcrowd the pan. Remove the scallops and keep warm. Pour the wine into the skillet to deglaze; reduce the wine by half, then add the reserved apple and shallot mixture. Bring to a boil and cook 1 minute; adjust seasoning. Return scallops to skillet; add butter cubes, stirring gently to melt butter and coat scallops.

To serve, arrange apple rings and scallops on plates; top with sauce and garnish with rosemary sprigs. *Serves 4.*

Wine suggestion: New Zealand Sauvignon Blanc

EGGPLANT AND CHÈVRE GRATIN

CHARLOTTE LANE CAFÉ, SHELBURNE, NS

Accompany this flavourful luncheon dish with melba toast, hot rolls or thick slices of crusty peasant bread. The recipe is easily converted to a first-course hot appetizer by simply reducing the size of the portions.

4 tablespoons balsamic vinegar

4 tablespoons raspberry vinegar

3 tablespoons granulated sugar

12 thin slices pancetta bacon*

8 slices eggplant, 3 inch/8 centimetres in diameter and ½ inch/1 centimetre thick

8 slices ripe tomato, 3 inch/8 centimetres in diameter and ½ inch/1 centimetre thick

6 ounces chèvre (goat's-milk cheese), thinly sliced

4 fresh herb sprigs of choice

Freshly ground pepper

*Pancetta is a salt- and brine-cured Italian bacon found in the deli section of most food stores. If unavailable, you may substitute regular smoked bacon, but the taste will be slightly different.

In a small saucepan, heat vinegars and sugar over medium-high heat, stirring frequently until reduced to a syrup, about 8 minutes. Reserve and keep warm.

Preheat oven to 350°F. In a skillet over medium heat, fry pancetta until crisp; reserve on paper towels to absorb excess fat. Sauté eggplant in bacon fat until soft and golden brown. To assemble, layer on a baking sheet: 2 slices of eggplant, topped with 3 slices of pancetta bacon and 2 slices of tomato. Bake for 5 to 7 minutes, until warmed through. Add cheese and place under the broiler until heated and cheese is soft. Transfer to serving plates, drizzle vinegar reduction over and around gratins; season with freshly ground pepper and garnish with herb sprigs. *Serves 4.*

MUSHROOM AND THYME RISOTTO WITH WHITE BALSAMIC JUS

THE BRIARS INN AND COUNTRY CLUB, JACKSONS POINT, ON

Executive Chef Trevor Ledlie uses local Ontario mushrooms as the flavour focus of his delectable risotto. Varieties such as white button, cremino, porcino, oyster, portobello, shiitake and chanterelle mushrooms are available in most supermarkets. Choose mushrooms that are fresh, firm and of even colour.

2 tablespoons extra-virgin olive oil

4 tablespoons butter, divided

1 cup diced red onion

1 bay leaf

2 cloves garlic, minced

2 cups Arborio rice (short-grained Italian rice)

2 cups white wine

5 cups chicken stock, heated

1 teaspoon white balsamic vinegar

Mushroom Mixture (recipe follows)

12 snow peas, sliced thin

1 yellow zucchini, seeded, diced and steamed*

1 tomato, seeded and diced

½ teaspoon jalapeno pepper, minced

1 teaspoon truffle oil (optional)

1 teaspoon fresh thyme, chopped

½ cup Grana Padano cheese, grated (or substitute Parmesan or Romano)

Salt and pepper to taste

White Balsamic Jus (recipe follows)

*In a covered bowl, microwave diced zucchini with 2 tablespoons of water on high for 2 minutes; drain and reserve.

In a saucepan, heat olive oil and 2 tablespoons of the butter over medium heat; add onion, bay leaf and garlic and cook, covered, for 2 minutes. Add rice and cook, stirring constantly, until grains are slightly transparent. Pour in wine, wait for bubbles to appear and add 1 cup of the stock and balsamic vinegar. Cook, stirring often, adding remaining stock ½ cup at a time, allowing rice to completely absorb liquid each time, for about 25 minutes or until rice is al dente (almost tender). Stir in Mushroom Mixture, snow peas, zucchini, tomato, remaining 2 tablespoons of butter, jalapeno, truffle oil, thyme and cheese; season with salt and pepper.

To serve, mound slightly on plates or in shallow bowls; drizzle with White Balsamic Jus and garnish with fresh thyme and additional cheese. *Serves 6.*

Wine suggestion: California Fumé Blanc

MUSHROOM MIXTURE

1 tablespoon butter

1 tablespoon olive oil

2 cups assorted mushrooms, stemmed and sliced

1 shallot, diced

¼ teaspoon garlic, minced

½ teaspoon jalapeno pepper, minced

1 tablespoon white wine

1 teaspoon fresh thyme, chopped

Salt and pepper to taste

In large skillet over medium heat, heat butter and oil. When butter begins to foam, add mushrooms and sauté 3 minutes; add shallot, garlic and jalapeno and sauté an additional 20 seconds. Deglaze pan with wine, stirring up brown bits. Add thyme; adjust seasoning with salt and pepper, remove from heat and reserve.

WHITE BALSAMIC JUS

1 cup white balsamic vinegar

½ cup chicken stock

¼ cup brown sugar

1 clove garlic, minced

In a small saucepan over medium heat, combine all of the ingredients, bring to a boil and reduce by half, about 10 to 12 minutes. *Makes ¾ cup of sauce.*

MIXED MUSHROOMS IN PUFF PASTRY (FUNGHI MISTI IN PASTA SFOGLIA)

LA PERLA, DARTMOUTH, NS

The chef at La Perla suggests that before you begin a recipe you should assemble all the ingredients and equipment to ensure that you have "mise en place" (everything in place). This practice helps the home chef cook with the ease of a professional. Phyllo pastry may be substituted for the puff pastry in this recipe. Simply follow the directions on the package for baking phyllo.

3 tablespoons butter, softened

1 large clove garlic, minced

2 tablespoons shallots, minced

1½ pounds/750 grams mixed mushrooms (such as shiitake, oyster, button and porcini), coarsely chopped or torn

1 tablespoon chopped fresh sage (or 1 teaspoon dried)

1 tablespoon lemon juice

¼ cup grated Grana Padano cheese (or other hard Italian cheese, such as Parmesan or Romano)

Salt and pepper to taste

8 ounces/250 grams commercial puff pastry

Egg-wash (1 egg beaten with 1 tablespoon water)

Salad greens to serve 4

Mornay Sauce (recipe follows)

Aged balsamic vinegar

In a large skillet, melt butter and garlic over low heat; add shallots and sweat until translucent. Add mushrooms and sage; cook over medium heat, stirring frequently until just cooked, about 5 minutes. Stir in lemon juice, cheese, salt and pepper; adjust seasoning, remove from heat and cool.

Preheat oven to 425°F. Roll out pastry to ¼-inch/5-millimetre thickness and cut into 4 squares. Place ¼ of the mushroom mixture in the centre of each square; brush the edges with egg-wash and fold "envelope-style" into packets. Place packets, seam side down, on baking sheet; brush tops with egg-wash and bake until golden brown, about 15 minutes.

To serve, place a small bed of greens on each of 4 large plates, drizzle greens with balsamic vinegar and spoon a pool of Mornay sauce beside the greens. Cut the pastries on the diagonal and place on the dish, creatively leaning them on the greens and sauce. *Serves 4.*

Wine suggestion: Italian Pinot Grigio

MORNAY SAUCE

2 tablespoons butter

2 tablespoons all-purpose flour

1 cup whole milk (3½% mf)

¼ cup grated Gruyere cheese

2 tablespoons grated Grana Padano cheese (or other hard Italian cheese)

In a small saucepan over medium heat, melt butter; add flour, combine and stir constantly for one minute. Whisk milk into flour mixture until smooth; bring to a boil and cook, stirring constantly until thickened. Remove from heat; add cheeses and stir until melted and combined. *Makes 1 cup sauce.*

DOLMADES WITH LEMON SAUCE

OPA GREEK TAVERNA, HALIFAX, NS

Warm stuffed grapevine leaves, or dolmades, are a traditional treat in Greek cuisine. At Opa Greek Taverna, the chef serves his dolmades accompanied by a creamy lemon sauce. Preserved grapevine leaves can be found, bottled in brine, at ethnic food markets, and should be refrigerated after opening.

40 preserved grapevine leaves

1 small onion, finely chopped

¾ cup green onions, finely chopped

1 pound/500 grams ground beef

⅛ cup uncooked rice

2 tablespoons parsley, chopped

2 teaspoons mint, chopped

1 teaspoon salt

½ teaspoon ground black pepper

1 large potato, peeled and thinly sliced

1 large tomato, thinly sliced

1 lemon, thinly sliced

Water to cover

¼ cup olive oil

Lemon Sauce (recipe follows)

Remove vine leaves from the jar and blanch in boiling water for 3 minutes; remove to a bowl of ice water, then drain well.

In a bowl, combine onion, green onions, beef, uncooked rice, parsley, mint, salt and pepper. Spread individual vine leaves on a work surface, shiny side down, and place 1½ tablespoons of the meat mixture toward the stem end. Roll once, fold in the sides and roll into a neat package; repeat with the remaining mixture.

Line the base of a heavy saucepan with potato and tomato slices and pack grapevine rolls on top, folded side down, closely together in rows. Top with lemon slices and additional vine leaves; cover with water and olive oil. Place a plate or weight on top to keep the rolls from coming apart during cooking. Bring to a boil, reduce heat and simmer 1½ hours or until tender. Drain, reserving cooking liquid, and keep warm. Serve with Lemon Sauce. *Yields 30 dolmades.*

1½ teaspoons all-purpose flour

1½ teaspoons butter

¾ cup reserved broth from cooked dolmades

1 egg, beaten

1½ teaspoons lemon juice

Salt and pepper to taste

LEMON SAUCE

Melt butter in saucepan and stir in flour; cook 2 minutes, stirring constantly. Stir in reserved broth from dolmades; bring to a boil. In a separate bowl, beat egg and lemon juice until frothy. Stir a little of the hot sauce into the egg to incorporate, then add to sauce. Continue to cook over medium heat, stirring until thickened, approximately 2 minutes. Serve warm with dolmades. *Makes 1 cup*.

HARVEST VEGETABLE POLENTA TORTE

INN ON THE LAKE, WAVERLEY, NS

Polenta is a hearty staple of northern Italian cuisine. At Inn on the Lake, Chef Scott Brown laces his polenta with autumn vegetables and serves it as a luncheon dish or an accompaniment with dinner.

1 cup green peppers, diced

2 tablespoons olive oil

1 cup fresh beets, cooked and diced

½ cup fresh corn kernels, cooked

½ cup fresh carrots, cooked and diced

1 cup whole milk (3½% mf)

1 cup chicken broth

2 cloves garlic, minced

3 sprigs fresh thyme

½ cup cornmeal

½ teaspoon salt

¼ teaspoon white pepper

2 eggs

½ cup freshly grated Parmesan cheese

Salt and pepper to taste

4 round corn tortillas or flatbreads, 9-inch/23-centimetre size

½ cup grated Monterey Jack cheese

Guacamole, salsa and sour cream for garnish

Early in the day, sauté green peppers in olive oil over medium heat until tender. Cover with plastic wrap and set aside. In separate bowls, set aside beets, corn and carrots.

In a large saucepan, bring milk, broth, garlic and thyme to a simmer. Turn off burner; steep for 20 minutes and remove thyme. Return mixture to a boil; slowly add cornmeal in a steady thin stream, stirring constantly, until cornmeal is incorporated, about 5 minutes. Stir in salt and pepper; reduce heat to very low, cover saucepan and allow to stand 10 minutes.

Remove polenta to a mixing bowl and stir in eggs, one at a time. Stir in the Parmesan cheese. Divide the polenta evenly into three bowls. To the first bowl, mix in the green peppers; to the second bowl, mix in the beets; to the third bowl, stir in the corn and carrots. Keep each bowl covered.

Preheat oven to 350°F. To assemble the torte, lightly oil a 9-inch/2-litre springform cake pan with butter or vegetable spray. Place a tortilla in the bottom of the pan and spread with the green pepper polenta. Top this layer with another tortilla and spread with the beet polenta. Top with another tortilla and spread with the corn and carrot polenta. Top with the last tortilla; sprinkle with Monterey Jack cheese. Cover pan with foil and bake 45 to 55 minutes, removing the foil for the last 15 minutes to allow the cheese to brown slightly. Remove from the oven and let stand 15 minutes before removing from the pan. Serve in wedges garnished with guacamole, salsa and sour cream. *Serves 6 to 8.*

Wine suggestion: Italian Primitivo

ROTINI WITH WILD FUNGI SAUCE

CHANTERELLE COUNTRY INN, NORTH RIVER, ST. ANNS BAY, NS

Blessed are the chefs with a supply of wild mushrooms on their property! Alas, most of us get our fungi at the grocery store, so we suggest that you use a variety of fresh mushrooms such as white button, Portobello, cremino, oyster or shiitake. Owner/chef Earlene Busch says the sauce is equally delicious served over chicken breast or steak.

2 tablespoons unsalted butter

1 tablespoon olive oil

2 shallots, finely chopped

1 clove garlic, minced

½ cup chunky tomato sauce

1 tablespoon Dijon mustard

½ pound/250 grams mixed mushrooms, cleaned and coarsely chopped

Salt and freshly ground pepper to taste

6 tablespoons red wine

2 tablespoons sherry

2 tablespoons parsley, chopped

½ cup heavy cream (35% mf)

Fresh chervil or parsley for garnish

3 to 4 cups rotini, prepared according to package directions

Heat butter and olive oil in a shallow saucepan over medium heat. Add shallots and garlic and sauté until vegetables are soft and golden. Stir in tomato sauce and mustard. Cook for 1 minute; add mushrooms and season with salt and pepper. Cook 2 minutes, stirring frequently. Stir in red wine, sherry, chopped parsley and cream. Simmer 10 minutes.

While sauce is cooking, prepare rotini al dente and drain. Serve sauce over rotini with a sprinkle of fresh chervil or parsley. *Serves 4.*

Wine suggestion: Italian Chianti

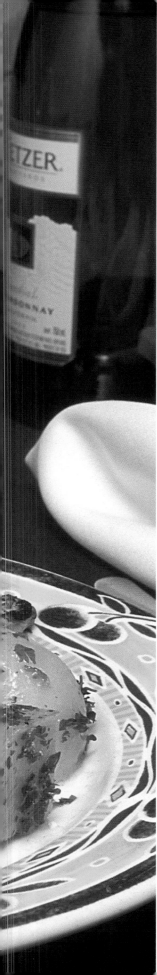

ENTREES

With the approach of autumn, our lives become more structured. The carefree days of summer are lost to school routines and the preparation of our psyches for the cold months of winter. There is so much to do and so little time to do it. Perhaps that is why it is so important for families and friends to gather together for an evening meal. Dinnertime should equate with relaxation and conversation, as well as provide nutrition for the body and soul.

Our contributing chefs have created a wonderful variety of flavours in their main-course recipes with an accent on fresh local ingredients such as salmon and scallops, chicken, pork and beef. Many of their recipes, such as Caramelized Sea Scallops with Bacon and Squash Risotto from Chef Craig Flinn, and Roasted Rack of Lamb with Sun-Dried Berry Port Wine Sauce from Chef Roland Glauser, offer bonus side-dish and sauce recipes. To help you with your entertaining plans, our wine consultant, John Vego, helped us choose complementary wines for each meal.

After you have chosen an entree, round out your meal with a soup, salad, side dish and dessert. As dinnertime approaches, set the table, warm the hearth, finish preparing the food and then sit back and relax.

◀ Chicken Lemonato with Shrimp

BACON-WRAPPED VEAL CHOPS WITH CRANBERRY CHUTNEY

HILLEBRAND'S VINEYARD CAFÉ, NIAGARA-ON-THE-LAKE, ON

Double-smoked bacon infuses an earthy flavour in these succulent veal chops. At Hillebrand's Vineyard Café, the chef serves this dish accompanied by freshly made cranberry chutney.

4 veal chops, 7 ounces/200 grams each

16 slices double-smoked bacon

Cracked black pepper to taste

Oil for browning

Cranberry Chutney (recipe follows)

Trim excess fat from chops and set aside. Place 4 slices of bacon, slightly overlapping, on a flat surface. Place one of the veal chops on the bacon so that only the meat touches the bacon and the bone is left exposed. Wrap the bacon over the top of the meat from each side, ensuring that the meat is fully covered and the bacon is as tight as possible. Season generously with cracked black pepper. Repeat procedure until all the chops are bacon-wrapped.

Preheat oven to 400°F. Heat an ovenproof skillet over medium-high heat, adding just enough oil to cover the bottom of the pan. Sear the chops on both sides, in batches, being careful not to crowd the pan. Finish the chops in the oven, cooking to desired doneness, about 8 minutes. Serve with Cranberry Chutney. *Serves 4.*

Wine suggestion: Italian Rosso di Montalcino

1 cup fresh cranberries

⅓ cup dried cranberries

2-inch/5-centimetre stick of cinnamon

1 teaspoon ground ginger

¼ teaspoon ground cloves

Pinch of nutmeg

Pinch of allspice

2 tablespoons sherry vinegar

3 tablespoons brown sugar

CRANBERRY CHUTNEY

Combine all ingredients in a heavy saucepan; bring to a boil, reduce heat and simmer, stirring frequently, until berries burst and the sauce thickens, about 10 minutes. Remove cinnamon stick and cool. *Makes 1½ cups of chutney.*

MAPLE-ROASTED PORK LOIN WITH CURRIED PINEAPPLE CHUTNEY

THE DUNDEE ARMS HOTEL, CHARLOTTETOWN, PEI

Chef Patrick Young at the Dundee Arms serves his succulent pork roast accompanied by Curried Pineapple Chutney and autumn root vegetables such as carrots, parsnips and pan-roasted potatoes.

4 pounds/1.8 kilograms pork loin roast, boneless and rolled

¾ cup pure maple syrup

Freshly ground black pepper

Curried Pineapple Chutney (recipe page 122)

Preheat oven to 350°F. Drizzle roast with maple syrup, turning to coat; season with freshly ground black pepper. Bake the pork loin, allowing 20 to 25 minutes per pound (45 minutes per kilogram), until it reaches an internal temperature of 160°F. Turn halfway through baking and baste with glaze. Remove from oven and tent with foil for 5 minutes. Slice and serve accompanied with Curried Pineapple Chutney. *Serves 6.*

Wine suggestion: New Zealand Sauvignon Blanc

PEPPERED BEEF TENDERLOIN

INN ON THE LAKE, WAVERLEY, NS

We enjoy sharing recipes that may be partially prepared in advance. This impressive steak entree is a good example because the sauce may be made earlier in the day and reheated at serving time. Five Peppercorn Blend is a combination of colourful peppercorns and is found in most supermarkets.

4 beef tenderloin filets, 6 ounces/175 grams each

Salt and pepper to season

1½ teaspoons vegetable oil

3 tablespoons Dijon mustard

¾ teaspoon Worcestershire sauce

¾ teaspoon dried rosemary, slightly crushed

2 to 3 teaspoons crushed Five Peppercorn Blend

Peppercorn Sauce (recipe follows)

Season beef filets with salt and pepper. Preheat a sauté pan on high with oil. Sear the beef, making sure to move the meat around in the pan, browning it on all sides. Remove the filets from the pan and let them rest for 10 minutes.

Preheat oven to 375°F. In a small bowl, combine mustard, Worcestershire sauce, rosemary and crushed peppercorns. Brush the mustard mixture over the beef and bake on a roasting rack, allowing 8 minutes for rare or 10 minutes for medium. Allow the meat to rest 5 minutes before serving on a pool of hot Peppercorn Sauce. *Serves 4.*

PEPPERCORN SAUCE

1 tablespoon butter

1 tablespoon shallots, finely chopped

1 teaspoon garlic, finely minced

1½ teaspoons green peppercorns, drained

3 tablespoons brandy

¾ teaspoon thyme

⅓ cup white wine

1½ cups beef stock

⅓ cup heavy cream (35% mf)

1 tablespoon cold butter

Melt butter over medium heat and sauté shallots, garlic and green peppercorns for 3 to 5 minutes. Increase heat, add brandy and ignite to flambé and burn off alcohol. Stir in the thyme and white wine and reduce by half. Add beef stock and bring to a boil, reduce by half. Stir in the cream and return to a boil. Reduce slowly until sauce thickens and coats the back of a wooden spoon. At serving time, return to a boil and whisk in 1 tablespoon of cold butter.

Wine suggestion: California Cabernet

FARM-RAISED VENISON CHOPS WITH WILD MUSHROOM RAGOUT

GABRIEAU'S BISTRO, ANTIGONISH, NS

This recipe features farm-raised venison and offers a delicious "hint of the wild." Venison steak or medallions are easily substituted for the rack of venison chops featured in the photo. The chef complements his dish with a thick ragout of wild mushrooms.

8 venison chops, 4 ounces/125 grams each

2 tablespoons vegetable oil

Salt and pepper

3 tablespoons pesto*

3 tablespoons Dijon mustard

1 cup dry bread crumbs

Wild Mushroom Ragout (recipe follows)

*Pesto is available in jars in the Italian section of grocery stores.

Trim chops of excess fat and rub lightly with oil; season with salt and pepper. Sear chops in a large skillet over medium-high heat, turning once; set aside. Preheat oven to 400°F. Combine pesto and mustard in a small bowl; spread on chops and pat with bread crumbs. Place on an oiled baking sheet and bake until medium rare, about 8 minutes. Serve chops on a bed of Wild Mushroom Ragout. *Serves 4.*

Wine suggestion: French Côtes du Rhône

1 tablespoon olive oil, divided

1 tablespoon butter, divided

1 cup sweet onion, diced

1 large clove garlic, minced

¼ teaspoon dried thyme leaves

1 tablespoon port wine

½ tablespoon soy sauce

¼ teaspoon cracked mixed peppercorns

1 cup each chanterelle, shiitake and oyster mushrooms, sliced

½ cup heavy cream (35% mf)

Salt and pepper

WILD MUSHROOM RAGOUT

In a skillet over medium-low heat, sauté onions, garlic and thyme in half the oil and butter until golden brown, about 20 minutes. Stir in port, soy sauce and cracked pepper; remove from heat and reserve.

Heat remaining olive oil and butter in a separate large skillet over medium-high heat; sauté mushrooms until fully cooked and lightly browned. Add onion mixture and cream to skillet; reduce heat to simmer and cook until reduced by half. Ragout should be thick and creamy. Adjust seasoning with salt and pepper to taste. *Serves 4.*

ROASTED RACK OF LAMB WITH SUN-DRIED BERRY PORT WINE SAUCE

CHARLOTTE LANE CAFÉ, SHELBURNE, NS

The sweet port wine sauce is a pleasing complement to the succulent herb-scented lamb ribs in this creation from Chef Roland Glauser.

2 tablespoons each of fresh rosemary and thyme, chopped (or 1½ teaspoons each dried)

½ teaspoon freshly ground pepper

½ teaspoon salt

1 teaspoon curry powder

Dash each of garlic powder, onion powder and paprika

2 racks of lamb, each 12 to 14 ounces/375 to 400 grams

1 tablespoon vegetable oil

Sun-Dried Berry Port Wine Sauce (recipe follows)

In a small bowl, combine herbs and seasoning; reserve. Trim fat from lamb but leave silver skin intact to crisp.

Preheat oven to 375°F. In an ovenproof skillet or roasting pan, heat oil over medium-high heat; briefly sear lamb racks on both sides. Remove from heat. Season with reserved herb mixture, pressing to adhere to meat. Bake 25 to 30 minutes for rare, or until desired doneness. Remove from oven and let stand for 5 minutes.

To serve, slice the lamb between the bones. Pour Sun Dried-Berry Port Wine Sauce in centre of warmed plates. Arrange 3 to 4 ribs per serving on a pool of sauce. Accompany with vegetables of choice. *Serves 4.*

Wine suggestion: Australian Shiraz

SUN-DRIED BERRY PORT WINE SAUCE

⅓ cup red currant jelly

2 tablespoons port wine

2 tablespoons red wine

5 tablespoons fresh orange juice

1 teaspoon fresh lemon juice

Zest from 1 orange and lemon

Pinch each of mustard powder, cayenne and ground ginger

½ cup dried berries (any combination of blueberry, cranberry or cherry)

2 teaspoons cornstarch dissolved in 1 tablespoon water

In small saucepan, combine all the ingredients except the cornstarch; bring to a boil, reduce heat to simmer and cook until the jelly is melted, stirring frequently. Add cornstarch mixture, stirring constantly until the sauce is slightly thickened. Keep warm. *Makes ¾ cup of sauce.*

HERB-RUBBED TURKEY WITH SHERRY GRAVY

The size of your Thanksgiving or Christmas turkey will depend upon the number of people gracing your dining room table. To calculate the size of turkey you'll need, allow 1 to 1½ pounds/500 to 680 grams of uncooked turkey per person (2 pounds/1 kilogram per person if the turkey weighs less than 10 pounds/4.5 kilograms). And if you love leftover turkey, be sure to increase the weight by a few pounds or kilos.

3 cups Turkey Stock (recipe follows)

2 tablespoons Herb Rub (recipe follows)

Seasoned Bread and Potato Stuffing (recipe page 94)

1 fresh 14-pound/6-kilogram turkey

4 tablespoons all-purpose flour

3 tablespoons dry sherry

Prepare Turkey Stock, Herb Rub and Seasoned Bread and Potato Stuffing in advance. Preheat the oven to 325°F. Rinse the turkey inside and out with cold water; pat dry with paper towels. Loosely stuff turkey cavities with Seasoned Bread and Potato Stuffing; close openings with skewers or sew with butcher's twine. Place the turkey on a rack set inside a large roasting pan and rub the exposed turkey skin with the Herb Rub.

Place the roasting pan on an oven rack set at the lowest position. Bake 1 hour and 15 minutes, covering the turkey loosely with foil if it's browning too quickly. Baste with pan drippings (if there are insufficient drippings, brush turkey with olive oil); cover with foil, shiny side down. Basting every 30 minutes, continue to bake the turkey an additional 3 hours or until a thermometer inserted into thickest part of the inner thigh registers 175°F. Remove foil during the last 30 minutes of baking, allowing the turkey to brown. Transfer turkey to a platter, tent with foil, and let stand 30 minutes before carving.

To make the gravy, skim all but 4 tablespoons of turkey fat from roasting pan. Place the roasting pan over 2 stove burners and make a roux by whisking 4 tablespoons of flour into the fat until smooth; cook and stir 3 minutes. Add sherry and Turkey Stock to roux and whisk until smooth. Bring to a boil and add any additional turkey juices from the platter; reduce heat and simmer until slightly thickened. Adjust seasoning and pour into gravy boat. *Serves 8.*

Wine suggestion: French Beaujolais

---

1 teaspoon dried oregano

1 teaspoon dried rosemary, crushed

1 teaspoon dried thyme

1 teaspoon dried sage

2 teaspoons sweet paprika

Pinch of ground ginger

¼ teaspoon salt

½ teaspoon freshly ground pepper

1 tablespoon olive oil

HERB RUB
This rub works well with poultry, pork and beef.

In a small bowl, combine all ingredients and stir to blend. *Makes 3 tablespoons of rub.*

TURKEY STOCK

If you prefer, make the stock the day before you bake the turkey. On special holidays such as Thanksgiving and Christmas, this will ease kitchen clutter and the chef's stress.

1 tablespoon olive oil

Neck and giblets (without the liver) from turkey, washed and dried

1 large carrot, chopped

1 medium red or sweet onion, chopped

1 stalk celery, chopped

Pinch of poultry seasoning

5 peppercorns

1 cup dry white wine

5 cups chicken stock, water or combination of both

In a large heavy-based pot, heat oil over medium-high heat until fragrant. Add neck and giblets and cook until browned, about 4 minutes. Add carrot, onion and celery and cook, stirring frequently until golden, about 5 minutes. Add seasoning, peppercorns and white wine; bring to a boil and cook 1 minute. Add stock and cook at a brisk simmer until reduced to 3 cups of liquid, about 30 minutes.

Remove stock from heat; strain and discard solids. Let cool to room temperature, skim off fat and impurities and reserve, covered, in the refrigerator. *Makes 3 cups of stock.*

CHICKEN LEMONATO WITH SHRIMP

OPA GREEK TAVERNA, HALIFAX, NS

Lemon is a common ingredient in Greek cuisine and this version of lemon chicken from Opa is not only delicious but also very appealing to the eye!

4 chicken breasts, boneless and skinless, 5 ounces/142 grams each

Flour for dredging

2 tablespoons unsalted butter, divided

12 thin slices lemon

1 medium red pepper, in julienne strips

12 large, raw shrimp, peeled

1 cup white wine

Salt and pepper

2 tablespoons freshly chopped parsley for garnish

Slice each chicken breast lengthwise into three pieces. Place between pieces of plastic wrap and pound to ¼-inch/5-millimetre thickness. Dredge chicken pieces in flour, shaking off excess. Melt 1 tablespoon of butter in a sauté pan over medium-high heat and brown chicken slices. Turn chicken, add lemon, red pepper strips and shrimp and sauté 2 minutes. Add wine and cook until chicken and shrimp are just done and juice has reduced slightly. To serve, place chicken slices on plates, top with lemon slices and shrimp. Return pan juices to a boil and whisk in remaining butter. Cook 1 minute and drizzle sauce over chicken. *Serves 4.*

Wine suggestion: Italian Pinot Grigio

SEAFOOD VOL-AU-VENT

GAFFER'S GOURMET BISTRO AT WHITEHALL COUNTRY INN, CLARENVILLE, NF

The spirit of this dish was certainly born in Atlantic Canada with its abundance of fresh seafood. You may substitute any combination of seafood in this recipe, such as crab, lobster and halibut.

1 sheet commercial puff pastry (½ of a 12-ounce/375-gram package)

1 tablespoon vegetable oil

1 tablespoon butter

⅓ pound/180 grams shrimp

⅓ pound/180 grams scallops

⅓ pound/180 grams salmon cut into 1-inch/2.5-centimetre cubes

4 canned artichoke hearts, quartered

8 small red potatoes, cooked with skin on (if large, cut into ½-inch/1-centimetre cubes)

¼ cup brandy

16 fresh mussels, scrubbed and debearded

¼ cup white wine

1 cup heavy cream (35% mf)

½ teaspoon cayenne pepper (or to taste)

Salt and pepper to taste

¼ cup grated Swiss cheese

¼ cup grated Cheddar cheese

Preheat oven to 400°F. Roll out pastry and cut into 4 pieces. Bake for 12 to 14 minutes until pastry is puffed and golden. Remove from oven and carefully separate the pastry in half to make a top and a bottom; return the pastry to the oven and bake an additional 1 to 2 minutes. Reserve.

Heat oil and butter in a large skillet over medium-high heat, add shrimp, scallops, salmon, potatoes and artichokes and sauté, stirring gently until shrimp turn pink. Add the brandy to the seafood, being careful that it does not flame; remove seafood from skillet and reserve. Add the mussels and wine to the skillet, cover and steam until the mussels open, about 5 to 6 minutes. Discard any mussels that do not open. If the wine evaporates before the mussels open, add more wine or water to the skillet. Remove the mussels and reserve. Add cream, cayenne pepper and any liquid from the cooked seafood to skillet; simmer over medium heat until thickened. Adjust seasoning with salt and pepper.

Place bottom half of puff pastries on each of 4 ovenproof dishes and arrange 4 mussels around each pastry. Portion the seafood onto the pastry, top with the sauce and grated cheeses and cap with the pastry tops. Bake in a 400°F oven until the cheese melts, about 5 minutes. *Serves 4.*

Wine suggestion: Pacific Northwest Pinot Gris

ARCTIC CHAR WITH ROASTED ROOT VEGETABLES

INN AT BAY FORTUNE, BAY FORTUNE, PEI

Delicate pink-fleshed arctic char has a flavour and texture that is a cross between trout and salmon. The chef at Inn at Bay Fortune serves his fish over roasted root vegetables with Truffled White Bean Froth.

4 fillets arctic char, 5 ounces/142 grams each

¾ cup each red potato, parsnip, carrot and turnip, pared and in medium dice

2 tablespoons olive oil

1 tablespoon fresh thyme, finely minced

1 large clove garlic, minced

Salt and pepper to taste

Truffled White Bean Froth (recipe follows)

2 tablespoons vegetable oil

Rinse and pat dry arctic char fillets and set aside. Preheat oven to 375°F. Toss diced potato, parsnip, carrot and turnip in olive oil. Sprinkle with thyme and garlic and season with salt and pepper. Roast in oven, stirring mixture every 10 minutes until tender and golden, about 35 minutes. Keep warm.

Preheat oven to 400°F. Sear fish, skin side down, in oil over medium-high heat until crust is formed, about 2 to 3 minutes. Finish fish in oven, until flesh is lightly pink and gives gently when pressure is applied after about 7 minutes.

Serve fish skin side up on a bed of roasted vegetables surrounded by Truffled White Bean Froth. *Serves 4.*

Wine suggestion: French White Burgundy

TRUFFLED WHITE BEAN FROTH

1 cup dried white beans (or 2 cups canned white beans, cannellini or garbanzo beans, drained and rinsed)

½ to ¾ cup hot chicken stock

1½ tablespoons truffle oil or extra-virgin olive oil

Salt and white pepper

Soak beans in water overnight to soften. Drain the beans and place in a heavy saucepan with enough water to cover. Bring beans to a boil, reduce heat to simmer and cook until tender; drain beans.

In a blender, purée beans and enough hot stock to create a smooth sauce of pouring consistency. Remove mixture to a small, deep bowl or 4-cup measuring cup. Stir in oil and adjust seasoning with salt and pepper to taste. With a hand mixer or blender, purée the beans until frothy. *Makes 1½ cups of froth.*

MINTED MAPLE-GLAZED SALMON

CASTLE ROCK COUNTRY INN, INGONISH FERRY, NS

The creation of Chef Jason Bailey, this easy-to-prepare salmon recipe calls for peppermint schnapps, which can be found in liquor stores, or peppermint extract, which can be found in the baking section of grocery stores.

4 salmon fillets, boneless and skinless, 5 ounces/142 grams each

Vegetable oil for searing

½ cup pure maple syrup

¾ teaspoon lemon juice

1 teaspoon peppermint schnapps or extract

Preheat oven to 425°F. Rinse and pat dry salmon fillets. In an ovenproof skillet over high heat, sear the salmon in a small amount of oil for 1 minute. Remove from the burner and turn the salmon fillets over. Mix together the maple syrup, lemon juice and peppermint extract in a small bowl. Drizzle the syrup over the salmon and bake 7 to 10 minutes until the fish is opaque and flakes easily with a fork. *Serves 4.*

Wine suggestion: Australian Chardonnay

BRAISED ATLANTIC SALMON WITH SUN-DRIED TOMATOES, LEEKS AND FENNEL

ARBOR VIEW INN, LUNENBURG, NS

Spectacular in its presentation, Chef Daniel Orovec of Arbor View Inn serves his salmon and sauce over garlic mashed potatoes, garnished with a fennel frond. To ensure even cooking, choose salmon fillets of equal thickness.

4 skinless salmon fillets, 6 ounces/175 grams each

Salt and pepper to season

2 tablespoons olive oil

2 tablespoons butter

⅓ cup chopped leeks, white part only and washed well

¼ bulb of fennel, finely sliced

½ cup sun-dried tomatoes in oil, drained and thinly sliced

1 to 2 cloves garlic, finely minced

½ cup dry white wine

Fennel fronds for garnish

Preheat oven to 400°F. Rinse and pat dry salmon fillets; season with salt and pepper. Heat olive oil and butter in a skillet over medium heat; add leeks, fennel and sun-dried tomatoes and sauté 1 minute. Add garlic and sauté, stirring constantly, until garlic becomes fragrant. Do not allow garlic to burn. Stir in the wine.

Place salmon fillets in skillet and sauté 1 minute. Carefully turn the salmon over and finish braising in the oven for 5 to 7 minutes, until the fish is opaque and flakes easily with a fork. Garnish plate with fennel fronds. *Serves 4.*

Wine suggestion: Pacific Northwest Pinot Gris

PECAN-CRUSTED TROUT WITH ORANGE BUTTER SAUCE

LA PERLA, DARTMOUTH, NS

Boneless trout fillets are available year-round, and you should choose ones of equal thickness. At La Perla, Chef James MacDougall serves his spectacular entree accompanied by saffron rice pilaf and garden fresh green beans.

4 trout fillets, 8 ounces/250 grams each

Flour for dredging

Salt and pepper to taste

2 egg whites, beaten with a whisk

¾ cup chopped pecans

1 tablespoon vegetable oil

2 teaspoons butter

Orange Butter Sauce (recipe follows)

Preheat oven to 350° F. Rinse and pat dry trout fillets. Dredge fillets in flour, shaking off excess; season with salt and pepper. Brush the flesh side of the fillets with egg white and crust with pecans. Heat oil and butter over medium-high and fry fish, flesh side down for about 30 seconds, then turn fillets over. Drain any excess oil from the pan and finish the fish in oven, allowing about 8 minutes, depending upon the thickness of the fish. Serve fish drizzled with Orange Butter Sauce. *Serves 4.*

Wine suggestion: Australian Chardonnay

½ cup fresh orange juice

¼ cup Bourbon whiskey

3 tablespoons butter

Salt and pepper to taste

ORANGE BUTTER SAUCE

In a small saucepan, heat orange juice over high heat; reduce volume by half. Remove saucepan from heat, add bourbon and carefully ignite to burn off the alcohol. Return pan to heat and cook until sauce is reduced by half again. Whisk in butter to create an emulsified sauce and season with salt and pepper to taste. *Makes ¾ cup.*

CARAMELIZED SEA SCALLOPS WITH BACON AND SQUASH RISOTTO

CHIVES CANADIAN BISTRO, HALIFAX, NS

Chef Craig Flinn of Chives Bistro serves his seared sea scallops on a bed of creamy risotto. His addition of double-smoked bacon and toasted pine nuts gives an earthy flavour to the rice, and while the directions for preparing the risotto are quite detailed, the results are well worth the effort.

1 cup butternut squash in small dice, blanched 2 minutes

½ cup double-smoked bacon, diced

¼ cup sweet onion, finely diced

1 cup Arborio rice

1 cup white wine

3 cups chicken or vegetable stock, heated

2 tablespoons toasted pine nuts*

2 tablespoons grated Parmesan cheese

1 tablespoon fresh sage, chopped

4 ounces/125 grams Swiss chard

3 tablespoons butter

1¼ pounds/567 grams sea scallops, rinsed and patted dry

*To toast pine nuts, place pine nuts on a baking sheet and roast in a 350°F oven for 5 minutes or until golden.

Blanch diced squash 2 minutes in boiling water; drain and reserve. In a skillet over medium heat, fry bacon bits until crisp; remove bacon and reserve. Add onion and squash to remaining bacon fat in skillet and sauté until browned; add rice and cook, stirring constantly, until grains are slightly transparent.

Pour in wine and stock in ½ cup increments; cook, stirring often and adding additional liquid only when rice has absorbed the previous amount. Continue this procedure until the rice is al dente and creamy, about 25 to 30 minutes. Add bacon, Parmesan cheese, pine nuts and sage to risotto; remove to a serving dish and keep warm.

In a saucepan, lightly steam Swiss chard in small amount of boiling water until barely wilted; drain, chop and reserve.

Heat the butter in a skillet over high heat; add scallops and sear, turning once. Scallops are ready to turn when they come away from the pan on their own, about 1 minute per side. To serve, centre a mound of risotto in a shallow soup plate, place scallops around the risotto and garnish with wilted Swiss chard. *Serves 4.*

Wine suggestion: California Fumé Blanc

SIDES

We must confess that we enjoy everything about autumn, including forays to farm markets and vegetable stands. We love to visit U-pick farms and meander through the rows of veggies, searching for most perfectly formed specimens. Yet the true harvest of autumn's bounty is direct and with purpose. Farmers race against impending frost to gather their crops, and consumers look for vegetables with flavours strong enough to complement the heartier fare of fall.

In this section you will find a tempting variety of recipes featuring squash, potatoes, root vegetables, cabbage and Brussels sprouts. At Saint John's Dufferin Inn the chef serves New Brunswick Potato Cake — a delightful side dish of potato, leek and chèvre cheese, while at Nova Scotia's Haddon Hall Resort Inn, the chef cooks his yellow-fleshed potatoes in chicken stock and whips them with browned butter and crème fraîche. Be sure to sample the Braised Red Cabbage with Apples and Onion, a dish that is an excellent accompaniment to roasted pork or poultry, or try Steamed Carrots with Dill Sauce — a simple-to-prepare dish with a beautiful visual presentation.

◀ Autumn Squash Casserole

BARLEY RISOTTO WITH AUTUMN SQUASH AND SWISS CHARD

HILLEBRAND'S VINEYARD CAFÉ, NIAGARA-ON-THE-LAKE, ON

This risotto variation uses pearl barley rather than Arborio rice as its main ingredient. The chef at Hillebrand's adds blanched squash cubes and fresh Swiss chard to enhance the colour and flavour of this dish.

2 cups pearl barley

1 cup cubed squash (½ inch cubes/1 centimetre)

5 large sprigs rosemary

5 large sprigs thyme

2 bay leaves

1 tablespoon white peppercorns

6 cups chicken stock (or vegetable stock)

1 head garlic, halved

2 tablespoons olive oil

1½ cups onion, chopped

½ cup celery, chopped

½ cup carrot, chopped

3 cloves garlic, minced

1 cup Swiss chard, cut into 4-inch/10-centimetre strips

4 tablespoons unsalted butter

½ cup grated Parmesan cheese

Salt and pepper to taste

Preheat oven to 375°F. On a baking sheet, toast the barley in the oven until golden brown, about 8 minutes. Reserve barley. In a saucepan of boiling water, blanch squash cubes until barely tender; drain and reserve.

Gently "bruise" the rosemary and thyme with the back of a knife and tie the sprigs together with butcher's twine. Place bay leaves and peppercorns in a cheesecloth bag. In a saucepan, bring stock, herbs and the half-head of garlic to a boil, reduce heat to low and keep hot.

Heat olive oil in a large sauté pan over medium heat; add onion, celery and carrot and sauté, stirring frequently until slightly soft, about 4 minutes. Add minced garlic and sauté 2 minutes; add toasted barley and sauté an additional 2 minutes. Stirring frequently, add hot stock, 1 cup at a time, waiting for the liquid to be mostly absorbed before adding more stock. Stop adding stock when the barley is tender but still slightly firm, about 40 minutes. The risotto should be very moist and creamy but not runny. Remove from heat, discard herb sprigs and bay leaves and stir in squash, Swiss chard, butter and Parmesan cheese. Adjust seasoning with salt and pepper to taste. *Serves 6.*

AUTUMN SQUASH CASSEROLE

SEAWIND LANDING COUNTRY INN, CHARLOS COVE, NS

Innkeepers Jim and Lorraine Colvin choose moist and sweet butternut squash for this dish, but other winter squash such as acorn, buttercup or hubbard may be used. Select squash that are heavy for their size with deep-coloured skin that is free of blemishes.

2 medium butternut squash, peeled and cubed to make 5 cups

¼ cup granulated sugar

½ cup butter

1 large egg, beaten

1 teaspoon vanilla

¼ cup milk

Pinch of nutmeg

3 tablespoons butter, melted

¼ cup brown sugar

¼ cup flour

½ cup pecans or walnuts, chopped

Pinch of cinnamon

Boil prepared squash until soft; drain thoroughly and mash with sugar and butter. In a bowl, combine egg, vanilla, milk and nutmeg. Mix egg mixture with squash and pour into a lightly greased 1-quart/1-litre casserole dish.

Preheat oven to 350°F. Prepare topping by mixing together the melted butter, brown sugar, flour, nuts and cinnamon. Sprinkle over squash and bake 30 minutes or until topping is golden brown. *Serves 4 to 6.*

RUTABAGA AND APPLE PURÉE

The hardy root vegetable rutabaga, or Swede, is commonly confused with its more delicate relative,°F the turnip. Traditionally served in autumn, it is often found in side-dish combinations and wholesome stews. It can be prepared a day ahead of serving and reheated in the oven.

2 pounds/1 kilogram rutabaga, peeled and cubed

3 medium apples, peeled, cored and sliced

¾ cup fresh orange juice (or apple cider)

3 to 4 tablespoons tablespoons butter, divided

1 tablespoon brown sugar

Salt and fresh ground pepper

1 small to medium apple, cored, sliced in ¼-inch/5-millimetre rounds

Pinch of ground cinnamon and brown sugar

Cook rutabaga in water until soft, about 30 to 40 minutes; drain. Cook apples in orange juice until softened, about 8 to 10 minutes. In a food processor, purée rutabaga, apples and juice until smooth. Stir in 2 tablespoons of butter, brown sugar and salt and pepper to taste; remove to a serving dish.

Melt 1 to 2 tablespoons of butter in a skillet over medium heat, add apple rings and sauté on both sides until soft and golden. Sprinkle rings with cinnamon and brown sugar and continue to sauté until caramelized. Creatively place the rings on top of the purée. Serve immediately. *Serves 6.*

This dish can be prepared in advance. Bring to room temperature and bake in 350°F oven for 20 to 30 minutes or until heated through.

ROASTED GARLIC, STILTON AND POTATO PAVÉ

GABRIEAU'S BISTRO, ANTIGONISH, NS

Potato Pavé is traditionally served in squares and is prepared well in advance of serving, making it an ideal accompaniment to any entree. Boil your potatoes up to a day prior to serving and chill thoroughly before grating.

1½ pounds/750 grams potatoes, cooked, peeled and grated

¾ cup blend cream (10% mf)

1 large egg

1 tablespoon roasted garlic*

3½ ounces/100 grams Stilton or Gorgonzola cheese

¼ cup Parmesan cheese

Pinch of ground rosemary

Pinch of nutmeg

Boil the potatoes early in the day in salted water. Preheat oven to 325°F. Cool and peel the potatoes; grate potatoes into a lightly greased 9-inch/2-litre square baking dish. Mix remaining ingredients in a blender and pour over the potatoes. Bake for approximately 1 hour or until firm and light brown on top. *Serves 6.*

*To roast garlic, steam a whole garlic bulb until tender, approximately 10 minutes. Toss in extra-virgin olive oil and bake at 400°F until golden brown, about 30 minutes. Squeeze soft garlic from the bulb with your fingers.

BRAISED RED CABBAGE WITH APPLES AND ONION

DUNCREIGAN COUNTRY INN, MABOU, NS

Colourful in its presentation, this braised cabbage dish is an excellent accompaniment to roasted pork or turkey.

1 large onion, thinly sliced

1 tablespoon vegetable oil

1 small red cabbage, core removed and very thinly sliced

½ cup chicken broth

2 teaspoons balsamic vinegar

2 firm red cooking apples

2 tablespoons cream sherry

¼ cup pure maple syrup

Over low heat, sauté sliced onion in oil, stirring frequently until caramelized. This procedure takes approximately 30 minutes. Set onion aside.

Over low heat, simmer thinly sliced cabbage in chicken broth and vinegar until cabbage is tender, about 45 to 50 minutes, stirring occasionally. Core apples and slice, unpeeled, into wedges; spread onions over cabbage and top with apple wedges. Drizzle with sherry and maple syrup and continue to cook, covered, 15 minutes. To serve, carefully ladle with a slotted spoon onto plates, trying not to disturb the layers. *Serves 4 to 6.*

ROASTED PEARL ONIONS AND CRANBERRIES WITH ROSEMARY AND PORT

BEILD HOUSE, COLLINGWOOD, ON

After creating this unique baked vegetable dish, the owners of Beild House never returned to making ordinary cranberry sauce with turkey dinners. The recipe may be prepared 1 or 2 days in advance and served warm as a vegetable or chilled as a condiment.

1½ pounds/750 grams pearl onions

6 cups fresh or frozen cranberries

½ cup port wine

⅔ cup brown sugar

2½ teaspoons ground rosemary

3 tablespoons butter

Salt and pepper to taste

In a large pot of boiling water, blanch onions for 2 minutes; drain and plunge in ice water. When the onions are cold, cut off the root end, push out the onion and discard the skin.

Preheat oven to 350°F. Place the onions in a single layer in a shallow baking dish, halving any large onions to create a uniform cooking size. Scatter the remaining ingredients over the top and bake until the onions are softened and the sauce is thickened and reduced, about 35 to 40 minutes. If necessary, cover the last 5 to 10 minutes to soften onions without losing too much moisture. Adjust seasoning. *Serves 6.*

SEASONED BREAD AND POTATO STUFFING

All chefs have their favourite poultry stuffing for special occasions. We find this combination of good quality bread mixed with potato, celery, onion, nuts, dried fruit and herbs makes for a pleasing flavour that enhances but never overpowers the delicate taste of poultry. If you choose to bake the stuffing in the poultry cavities, pack it loosely and cook stuffing to 165°F.

2 tablespoons olive oil

2 tablespoons butter

1½ cups celery, diced

1½ cups onion, diced

4 cups day-old, rustic bread, torn into pieces

3 cups mashed potato

1½ cups dried mixed fruit, chopped (apple, apricot, prune, cranberry, etc.)

1 cup pecan pieces

1 tablespoon dried summer savory or sage (or to taste)

Salt and freshly ground pepper

¼ to ½ cup chicken stock

Heat olive oil and butter in a skillet over medium-low heat; add celery and onion and sauté until softened, about 8 minutes. Remove onion and celery to a large bowl; add the bread, potato, mixed fruit, pecans and savory or sage, and gently toss to combine. Add chicken stock, 2 tablespoons at a time, tossing the ingredients until stuffing is slightly moist. Add salt and freshly ground pepper and adjust seasoning. Cover and cool until ready to use.

Preheat oven to 350°F. Lightly spoon dressing into a greased casserole and bake for 45 minutes, until heated through and lightly crisped on top. *Makes 8 cups of stuffing.*

NEW BRUNSWICK POTATO CAKE

THE DUFFERIN INN AND SAN MARTELLO DINING ROOM, SAINT JOHN, NB

Easily prepared in advance, this Potato Cake is delicious served with beef or pork entrees. Saint Marie goat cheese has a mild flavour and is similar in texture to soft cream cheese. The chef says heavy cream may be substituted for the goat cheese.

1¼ pounds/625 grams Yukon Gold potatoes, peeled and thinly sliced

1 leek, white part only, washed and sliced

⅓ pound/170 grams Saint Marie goat cheese or ¾ cup heavy cream (35% mf)

3 eggs

Salt and pepper to taste

1 sprig fresh rosemary

Pastry (recipe follows)

Line a greased 8-inch/2-litre pie plate with pastry and set aside. Cook potatoes in boiling, salted water for 4 minutes; add leeks and continue to cook 1 minute. Drain thoroughly and cool.

Preheat oven to 375°F. Layer cooled potatoes and leeks in pie shell. Using an electric mixer, cream goat cheese and add eggs, one at a time; season mixture with salt and pepper. Pour over potatoes, being sure to cover completely. Sprinkle with fresh rosemary and bake 50 minutes or until vegetables are soft and golden brown. *Serves 6 to 8.*

¾ cup all-purpose flour

¼ teaspoon salt

⅓ cup unsalted butter

2 tablespoons cold water

1 small egg

PASTRY

Combine flour and salt in a bowl. Using a pastry blender or two knives, cut in butter. In a separate bowl, whisk together water and egg. Add to flour mixture, stirring to bind. Wrap in plastic wrap and chill 1 hour. Roll out on a floured surface and line a greased 8-inch/2-litre pie plate. Crimp edges and set aside.

STEAMED CARROTS WITH DILL SAUCE

Carrots are harvested in early autumn and you should choose straight carrots of equal size. If fresh dill is not available, substitute ½ teaspoon dried dill.

1½ pounds/750 grams fresh carrots, trimmed and peeled

3 tablespoons butter

2 teaspoons fresh dill, chopped

1½ tablespoons heavy cream (35% mf)

Salt and freshly ground pepper to taste

Slice carrots into uniform thickness and steam until crisp-tender, approximately 5 minutes. Melt butter in a saucepan and sauté carrots for 1 minute, tossing to coat. Stir in dill and cream and heat through, about 2 minutes; season with salt and pepper. *Serves 4.*

OVEN-BAKED BEANS

LISCOMBE LODGE, LISCOMB MILLS, NS

Baked beans can be served as a side to breakfast, lunch or dinner. This recipe came to us from the chefs at Liscombe Lodge, where it is part of the breakfast menu.

1 pound/500 grams dry white beans, rinsed and cleaned

6 cups cold water

6 slices bacon, cut into 2-inch/5-centimetre pieces

1 small onion, chopped

½ teaspoon dry mustard

1½ teaspoon salt

½ cup pure maple syrup

2 tablespoons brown sugar

2 tablespoons butter

Bring the beans and water to a boil in a large saucepan and boil for 2 minutes. Remove from heat and let stand, covered, for an hour. Return to a boil, reduce heat and simmer, covered, for 40 minutes or until beans are fork tender. Drain, reserving cooking liquid.

Preheat oven to 325°F. Place half of the bacon in a bean crock and add the beans and onion. In a separate bowl, combine the reserved cooking liquid, dry mustard, salt and maple syrup. Pour over the beans and top with remaining bacon. Bake, covered, for about 3 hours, checking occasionally and adding a bit of water if the beans appear dry.

Cream together the brown sugar and butter. Sprinkle over the beans and bake, uncovered, an additional hour. *Serves 6 to 8.*

DESSERTS

There are those who purchase cookbooks simply to add new desserts to their repertoire and if you fall into that category, you will not be disappointed. Indeed, we have included desserts that range from traditional to decadent.

Treat your family to old-fashion Maple-Baked Apples or Harvest Blueberry Tarts, the creation of the owner/chef at the Dufferin Inn. Wow the crowd at Thanksgiving dinner with Spirited Pumpkin Mousse Cake — we are sure it will become an annual favourite. Harvest fresh autumn plums for gentle poaching in elegant Red Wine Plum Compote or sample Almond Cranberry Torte, an innovative dessert from Chef Roland Glauser of Charlotte Lane Café.

Several of these dishes include additional sauces and we encourage you to mix and match these delights with fresh fruit, ice cream or your own favourite dessert. Whether your dessert selection is the finale to a special dinner or a simple treat to satisfy a sweet tooth, we are sure you will enjoy our selection.

◀ Apple, Pear and Sun-Dried Cranberry Strudel with Maple Cream

COCONUT CARROT CAKE WITH CREAM CHEESE AND WHITE CHOCOLATE ICING

REBAR, VICTORIA, BC

This rendition of carrot cake defies tradition by incorporating smooth white chocolate within the yummy cream cheese icing. Consider topping the cake with a garnish of crushed nuts.

1½ cups carrot, grated

¾ cup crushed pineapple, drained

¾ cup unsweetened coconut

¾ cup chopped walnuts

½ cup chopped dates

¾ cup brown sugar

⅛ cup granulated sugar

3 eggs

2 teaspoons vanilla

¾ cup vegetable oil

1½ cups all-purpose flour

1½ teaspoons cinnamon

2 teaspoons baking powder

1 teaspoon baking soda

¼ teaspoon salt

1½ teaspoons ground ginger

½ teaspoon freshly grated nutmeg

½ teaspoon allspice

Cream Cheese and White Chocolate Icing
(recipe follows)

Preheat oven to 350°F. Butter and flour two 8-inch/2-litre round cake pans and set aside.

In a large bowl, combine carrot, pineapple, coconut, dates and walnuts. In a separate mixing bowl, beat sugars with eggs. Stir in vanilla and whip on high until the volume has tripled. Reduce mixer speed to low and blend in the vegetable oil.

In another bowl, combine the dry ingredients and gently stir into egg mixture. Fold in carrot mixture and divide batter between cake pans, smoothing the tops with a rubber spatula. Bake 30 minutes or until a toothpick inserted in the cake comes out clean. Loosen edges and turn out onto wire racks to cool.

Spread the bottom cake layer with one third of the icing, smoothing evenly to the edges. Chill 10 minutes. Place the top cake layer on the bottom and ice the sides and top. Refrigerate covered, up to 3 days. *Serves 12.*

CREAM CHEESE AND WHITE CHOCOLATE ICING

8 ounces/250 grams cream cheese, at room temperature

¼ cup unsalted butter, softened

1 teaspoon vanilla

3 ounces/85 grams white baking chocolate

3 cups icing sugar, sifted

Zest of one lemon, finely grated (optional)

Beat the cream cheese on high until smooth and fluffy. Lightly blend in butter and vanilla. Melt the white chocolate in a double boiler over medium heat. Add the hot melted chocolate to the cream cheese mixture. Scrape down the sides of the bowl and mix on high until smooth and fluffy. Slowly add the icing sugar and beat on high until all the sugar is incorporated and the icing is light and fluffy, about 3 minutes. Stir in lemon zest, if desired.

CHOCOLATE POTATO CAKE

CHANTERELLE COUNTRY INN, NORTH RIVER, ST. ANNS BAY, NS

The name of this cake certainly does not do it justice, for it is moist, fine textured and flavoured with a hint of cinnamon and nutmeg. You will find yourself peeling an extra potato or two for the evening meal just to have some leftover for the cake.

1 cup butter, softened

2 cups granulated sugar

4 eggs

3 ounces/85 grams unsweetened baking chocolate (or ⅔ cup cocoa, sifted)

1 cup cold mashed potatoes

1 teaspoon ground cinnamon

¼ teaspoon ground nutmeg

2 cups all-purpose flour

1 teaspoon baking soda

1 cup sour milk or 1 cup buttermilk

1 cup chopped walnuts or pecans

Chocolate Cocoa Icing (recipe follows)

In large mixing bowl, cream together butter and sugar until light and fluffy. Add eggs, one at a time, and continue to beat until well blended. In a double boiler over simmering water, melt chocolate; set aside and cool slightly. Preheat oven to 350°F. Add chocolate, potatoes, cinnamon and nutmeg to mixture and blend. Sift flour and baking soda together and add to batter alternately with sour milk in 3 batches. Stir in nuts and pour into greased and waxed-paper-lined 9-inch/2-litre square baking pan. Bake in oven for 45 to 50 minutes or until toothpick inserted in centre comes out clean. Cool on wire rack, remove from pan and spread with icing. *Serves 8 to 10.*

1¾ cups icing sugar

3 tablespoons cocoa

2 tablespoons butter, softened

2 tablespoons milk

½ teaspoon vanilla

Pinch of salt

CHOCOLATE COCOA ICING

Sift together the icing sugar and cocoa. In a food processor or mixing bowl, combine all ingredients and beat until smooth, scraping down bowl often. If necessary, add more milk to get desired consistency. Spread icing over top of cake, letting it drizzle down the sides.

RED WINE PLUM COMPOTE

LITTLE SHEMOGUE COUNTRY INN, PORT ELGIN, NB

Pungent fruit and wine flavours paired with hints of spice make this compote a favourite "adult" dessert.

6 large ripe red or blue plums

1½ cups dry red wine (preferably Merlot or Syrah)

1 cup granulated sugar

2 whole cloves

1-inch/2.5-centimetre cinnamon stick

Fresh whipped cream (optional)

French vanilla ice cream (optional)

Cut plums in half, remove pits and place skin side up in a large saucepan. Combine wine, sugar and spices in a bowl; stir to dissolve sugar. Gently pour wine mixture into saucepan and bring to a boil over medium-high heat. Reduce heat and lightly cook plums, being careful not to boil, for 15 to 18 minutes, until fruit has softened. Remove plums and sauce to a serving dish; discard cinnamon stick and cloves.

Plums may be served warm, cool or cold. Divide fruit and sauce between dessert bowls and garnish with ice cream and whipped cream. *Serves 6.*

CARAMELIZED APPLE AND NUT TART WITH ROASTED PEAR SORBET

WESTOVER INN, ST. MARYS, ON

The chefs at Westover Inn usually make a sweet dough for their tart shells, but they advise buying shells from the frozen food section of the grocery store, which otherwise work well for the home cook. The tarts may be made a day ahead, allowed to cool completely and then refrigerated overnight. They should be brought to room temperature before serving and warmed slightly in a 300°F oven for about 10 minutes.

8 sweet tart shells, 3-inch/8-centimetre size

¼ pound/125 grams mixed nuts (almonds, cashews and hazelnuts), coarsely chopped

4 Red Delicious apples, peeled, cored and cut into ¾-inch/2-centimetre cubes

4 tablespoons butter

⅓ cup granulated sugar

Roasted Pear Sorbet (recipe follows)

Raspberry coulis or whipped cream (optional)

Preheat oven to 325°F. Place tart shells in their foil cups on a baking tray. Divide the nuts among the shells and bake until shells and nuts are a light brown, about 10 minutes. Cool on a baking rack.

Prepare apples and set aside. Over medium heat, melt the butter in a heavy-bottomed saucepan. Sprinkle with sugar and do not stir. Immediately place apple pieces in the pan and spread out evenly over the whole surface. Allow apples to simmer 8 to 10 minutes.

Lower heat to medium-low and gently stir, turning apples over in the butter. Continue to cook, stirring every 5 minutes until apples are soft and golden brown. Remove from heat and divide the apples among the tart shells.

Return tarts to 375°F oven and bake until golden, approximately 10 to 12 minutes. Remove from oven, cool on a baking rack and gently remove foil cups. Serve with a scoop of Roasted Pear Sorbet and garnish with raspberry coulis or whipped cream. *Serves 8.*

3 pears (Bartlett or Anjou)

1 teaspoon olive oil

½ cup simple syrup*

1 teaspoon lemon juice

½ tablespoon pear liqueur (optional)

1 cup soda water

*To make a simple syrup, mix together ½ cup granulated sugar and ½ cup of water and bring to a boil. Immediately pour into a container and allow to cool.

ROASTED PEAR SORBET
You may make this sorbet up to a week ahead of time as long as you store it in the freezer in a well-sealed plastic container. Served on its own and garnished with a sprig of mint, this recipe makes a refreshing and elegant dessert.

Preheat oven to 400°F. Peel pears, slice in half and remove core. Cut each half into 3 wedges. Pour oil in a glass pie plate and add pear slices, tossing to cover with oil. Roast in oven for 30 minutes, stirring occasionally.

Remove from oven and allow to cool. Purée pears in a food processor and place purée in a 3- to 4-quart/3- to 4-litre stainless steel mixing bowl. Add syrup, lemon juice, liqueur and soda water; stir with a wire whisk.

If you have an ice-cream maker, freeze the sorbet according to the instructions; if not, place the bowl in the freezer and whisk every half hour for 3 hours. Place in a plastic container with a well-fitted lid and allow to freeze solid.

ALMOND CRANBERRY TART

CHARLOTTE LANE CAFÉ, SHELBURNE, NS

This wonderfully rich tart lends itself to a variety of fresh fruit. Simply choose the very best of the season: spring rhubarb, summer berries, or your choice of plums, cranberries, pears or apples in late summer and fall. At Charlotte Lane Café, the tarts are served with Raspberry Coulis and Crème Fraîche, but feel free to garnish with sweetened whipped cream.

Pastry:

1⅔ cups all-purpose flour

3 tablespoons granulated sugar

½ cup butter, softened

1 egg, beaten

Filling:

½ cup less 1 tablespoon butter, softened

½ cup granulated sugar

2 eggs

1 tablespoon lemon zest

¾ cup ground almonds

1 tablespoon all-purpose flour

⅓ cup raspberry jam

1 cup fresh cranberries

⅓ cup sliced almonds

Icing sugar for dusting

Raspberry Coulis (recipe follows)

Crème Fraîche (recipe follows)

In a large bowl, combine flour and sugar. Add butter and mix with fingertips until mixture resembles fine crumbs. Add egg and work into dough. Form into a disc, wrap in plastic wrap and let it rest in the refrigerator for 30 minutes.

On a lightly floured surface, roll out the dough to an ⅛-inch/3-millimetre thickness. Fit into a 10-inch/25-centimetre tart mold with removable bottom.

With mixer, cream butter, sugar and eggs until smooth. Stir in lemon zest; add ground almonds and flour and mix until well blended. Reserve.

Preheat oven to 350°F. Spread raspberry jam over pastry base. Cover jam with almond mixture, spreading to the edges of the tart. Sprinkle the cranberries over top, pressing lightly into filling; sprinkle with sliced almonds. Bake for 10 minutes; rotate pan, lower oven to 325°F and bake an additional 40 minutes, until golden and lightly puffed. Cool before removing from pan.

To serve, cut into portions, place on individual dessert plates and reheat 20 seconds in the microwave to lightly warm. Dust with icing sugar and garnish with raspberry coulis and a dollop of crème fraîche or whipped cream. *Serves 10.*

RASPBERRY COULIS

3 cups fresh or frozen unsweetened raspberries
⅓ cup granulated sugar or to taste
1 tablespoon cornstarch
1 tablespoon water

In a saucepan over medium heat, combine raspberries and sugar; bring to a boil, reduce heat to simmer and cook, stirring frequently, 3 to 4 minutes. Strain sauce through sieve to remove seeds and return raspberry juice to saucepan. Bring back to simmer; add cornstarch diluted in water and stir until slightly thickened. Cool, covered. *Makes ⅔ cup.*

CRÈME FRAÎCHE

If you're unable to find crème fraîche, make this inexpensive version at home.

½ cup cream (35% mf)
1 tablespoon buttermilk

In a glass container combine cream and buttermilk. Stir, cover and let stand at room temperature for 12 to 24 hours or until thickened. Stir and refrigerate until ready to use. *Makes ½ cup.*

SPIRITED PUMPKIN MOUSSE CAKE

This dessert, which is not quite a cheesecake and not quite a pumpkin pie, has a wonderful flavour and is a nice alternative to traditional Thanksgiving desserts.

1½ cups puréed pumpkin

½ cup heavy cream (35% mf)

½ cup granulated sugar

3 egg yolks, beaten

¾ teaspoon cinnamon

½ teaspoon ground ginger

¼ teaspoon ground nutmeg

¼ teaspoon ground allspice

¼ teaspoon salt

4 teaspoons unflavoured gelatin

¼ cup orange flavoured liqueur, e.g., Grand Marnier or Cointreau

3 egg whites

Pinch of cream of tartar

Pinch of salt

⅓ cup granulated sugar

Vanilla Wafer Crust (recipe follows)

Orange zest for garnish

In a saucepan, combine pumpkin, cream, sugar, beaten egg yolks, cinnamon, ginger, nutmeg, allspice and salt; whisk until smooth. Cook over medium heat, stirring occasionally, for 10 minutes. While pumpkin mixture is cooking, prepare gelatin. In the top section of a double boiler, sprinkle the gelatin over the liqueur and let it rest 5 minutes. Place top section of double boiler over simmering water and stir gelatin until dissolved. Transfer pumpkin mixture to a bowl, add gelatin and stir to combine; cool.

With a mixer, beat egg whites and cream of tartar until soft peaks form. With mixer running, add sugar, 2 tablespoons at a time, and beat until stiff peaks form. Fold egg whites into pumpkin mixture and pour into prepared Vanilla Wafer Crust. Cover and chill at least 6 hours.

To serve, unmold mousse cake onto serving plate. Cut cake into wedges, top with whipped cream and garnish with orange zest. *Serves 8 to 10.*

VANILLA WAFER CRUST

2 cups vanilla wafer crumbs (or graham cracker crumbs)

¼ cup granulated sugar

6 tablespoons butter, melted and cooled

Preheat oven to 400°F. In a bowl, combine vanilla wafer crumbs, sugar and melted butter; press into bottom and sides of 9-inch/2-litre springform pan. Bake for 10 minutes. Cool completely before filling.

APPLE CRISP WITH RUM RAISIN COULIS

INN ON THE LAKE, WAVERLEY, NS

At the Inn on the Lake, Chef Scott Brown allows the seasons to influence his menu and he serves Apple Crisp as soon as the first crop of firm apples are harvested. He creatively decorates his plate with small dollops of coulis topped with a drop of whipped cream.

3 to 4 firm apples (Granny Smith, McIntosh, Cortland, etc.)

2 tablespoons butter

2 tablespoons brown sugar

2 tablespoons granulated sugar

2 tablespoons brandy

½ teaspoon cinnamon

Pinch of nutmeg

1 tablespoon butter

3 tablespoons all-purpose flour

3 tablespoons rolled oats

3 tablespoons brown sugar

Rum Raisin Coulis (recipe follows)

Peel and core apples, then dice into ½-inch/1-centimetre cubes. Melt butter in a skillet over medium heat, add sugars and stir until dissolved. Add apples and brandy, stirring to coat apples in sugar mixture and cook 5 minutes. Remove from heat and stir in cinnamon and nutmeg. Divide among 4 buttered individual baking ramekins or a 1-quart/1-litre baking dish and set aside.

Preheat oven to 375°F. In a small bowl, combine butter, flour, rolled oats and brown sugar with fingers until mixture is crumbly. Sprinkle over apples and bake 30 to 40 minutes until top is golden brown. Serve warm with Rum Raisin Coulis. *Serves 4.*

½ cup seedless sultana raisins

⅓ cup granulated sugar

¼ cup rum

¼ teaspoon cinnamon

RUM RAISIN COULIS

Combine all ingredients in a saucepan and bring to a boil. Immediately lower heat, cover saucepan and simmer 30 minutes or until raisins are soft. Transfer to a blender and purée until smooth.

MAPLE-BAKED APPLES

Not all apples are created equal; some are ideal for eating fresh, some make delicious pies and sauces, while others are perfect for baking. This recipe works well with Cortland, Jonagold, Rome, Spy and Granny Smith varieties.

6 baking apples (about 2½ to 3 pounds/1.25 to 1.5 kilograms)

⅓ cup brown sugar

2 tablespoons chopped walnuts or pecans

2 tablespoons chopped raisins

Pinch each of ground cardamom, nutmeg and cinnamon

1 tablespoon butter

2 tablespoons water

⅓ cup pure maple syrup

Vanilla ice cream or whipped cream for garnish (optional)

Wash, dry and core apples. With a paring knife, make a shallow cut around the middle of each apple; place apples in a shallow baking dish.

Preheat oven to 400°F. In a bowl, mix together brown sugar, nuts, raisins and spices. Portion equal amounts of sugar and nut mixture in apple cavities. Dab apples with butter and pour water around apples. Bake for 35 minutes; drizzle maple syrup over apples and continue baking until apples are tender, about 10 minutes longer. Test for doneness with a toothpick; if it goes in smoothly the apple is cooked.

Place a warm or cooled apple in an individual serving-bowl and top with a spoonful of the maple sauce. Garnish, if desired, with vanilla ice cream or whipped cream. *Serves 6.*

HARVEST BLUEBERRY TARTS

THE DUFFERIN INN AND SAN MARTELLO DINING ROOM, SAINT JOHN, NB

Wild blueberries are a popular fruit and owner/chef Axel Bergner of the Dufferin Inn uses pure maple syrup to sweeten these delightful little tarts. In testing, we used both fresh and frozen berries with equal results. If using frozen berries, thaw slightly and extend the baking time.

8 to 10 small tart shells (recipe follows)

5 teaspoons brown sugar

1 teaspoon cinnamon

2 teaspoons cornstarch

2 cups wild blueberries

1 tablespoon pure maple syrup or maple liqueur

Whipped cream and mint leaves for garnish (optional)

Prepare pastry and line 3-inch/8-centimetre tart pans. Preheat oven to 375°F. In a small bowl, stir together the brown sugar, cinnamon and cornstarch. Add blueberries and toss to coat. Drizzle with maple syrup or liqueur and divide between tart shells. Bake in oven until fruit is bubbly and crust has browned, about 35 to 40 minutes. Cool and serve at room temperature, garnished, if desired, with a dollop of whipped cream and mint leaves. *Makes 8 to 10 small tarts.*

1 cup all-purpose flour

Pinch of salt

1 teaspoon baking powder

3 tablespoons sugar

½ cup unsalted butter

1 egg, beaten

TART PASTRY

Combine flour, salt, baking powder and sugar. Using a pastry blender, cut in butter. Stir in egg. Roll dough into a ball and wrap in plastic wrap. Chill one hour, then roll on a floured surface and cut into 4-inch/10-centimetre circles to line tart pans.

APPLE, PEAR AND SUN-DRIED CRANBERRY STRUDEL WITH MAPLE CREAM

GABRIEAU'S BISTRO, ANTIGONISH, NS

Sample the best of the autumn harvest rolled into one, actually, two strudels! At Gabrieau's Bistro the chef serves his warm strudel napped with a creamy custard sauce and fresh fruit.

1 package frozen puff pastry, 397 grams/14 ounces

1½ large apples (Granny Smith, Cortland or McIntosh)

1½ pears

1 cup dried cranberries

½ cup currants

⅓ cup crushed walnuts

⅓ cup crushed pecans

½ cup cubed firm white bread, crusts removed

¼ cup granulated sugar

¼ cup brown sugar

1 teaspoon cornstarch

2 tablespoons dark rum

2 teaspoons vanilla

Egg-wash (1 egg white whisked with 1 teaspoon water)

1 tablespoon granulated sugar for sprinkling

Maple Cream Sauce (recipe follows)

Remove puff pastry from freezer and thaw at room temperature for 2 hours or overnight in the refrigerator. Roll out each block on a floured board into two 12-inch/30-centimetre squares.

Preheat oven to 400°F. Peel and core the apples and pears and finely slice. Cover cranberries and currants with boiling water and let stand 5 minutes. Drain. In a large bowl, combine apples, pears, cranberries, currants, walnuts, pecans and bread cubes. Sprinkle with sugars, cornstarch, rum and vanilla, tossing to coat.

Place half the fruit mixture in a long row on each pastry square. Moisten edges of pastry with egg-wash, fold over the pastry and crimp edges on three sides to seal. Brush tops with egg-wash and sprinkle with sugar. Bake on a lightly greased baking sheet 35 to 40 minutes or until golden brown. Serve warm with Maple Cream Sauce. *Makes 2 strudels.*

1½ cups blend cream (10% mf)

3 egg yolks

2 tablespoons pure maple syrup

1 teaspoon cornstarch

1 teaspoon vanilla

MAPLE CREAM SAUCE

Scald cream by bringing almost to a boil. In a separate bowl, whisk together the egg yolks, maple syrup, cornstarch and vanilla. Slowly pour half the hot cream into the egg mixture, stirring constantly. Return eggs to the remaining cream and cook slowly over medium heat, stirring constantly until sauce thickens slightly and coats the back of a wooden spoon. Strain and chill. *Makes 1½ cups of sauce.*

PUMPKIN AND CRANBERRY BREAD PUDDING

CHIVES CANADIAN BISTRO, HALIFAX, NS

Comfort food, with a twist! Chef Craig Flinn of Chives Bistro marries the smooth taste of autumn pumpkins with tart cranberries and sweet maple syrup. Prepare this dish early in the day and pop it into the oven just before serving time. As an added treat the chef serves his dessert with a scoop of ice cream!

½ pound/250 grams day-old bread, cut into small dice

1 cup cranberries

½ cup blend cream (10% mf)

½ cup whole milk (3½% mf)

2 egg yolks

1 whole egg

¼ cup brown sugar

⅓ cup pumpkin purée

1½ teaspoons pumpkin pie spice

Cranberry Compote (recipe follows)

Orange Maple Glaze: Zest of 1 orange, ½ cup pure maple syrup

Ice cream and mint leaves for garnish (optional)

Place bread cubes and cranberries in a large bowl and set aside. In a separate bowl whisk together the remaining ingredients and pour over bread cubes, mixing thoroughly. Pour into a greased 9-inch/2-litre square baking pan, cover with plastic wrap and refrigerate several hours.

Preheat oven to 350°F. Place baking dish in a shallow pan, adding hot water around it to a depth of 1 inch/2.5 centimetres. Bake until custard has set and pudding is brown on top, approximately 45 minutes. To make the glaze, add orange zest to maple syrup in a saucepan and bring to a boil. Remove from heat, cover and let steep. Cool to room temperature. *Makes ½ cup of glaze.*

Cut into squares and serve, warm, with a tablespoon of Cranberry Compote and garnish with fresh mint leaves and ice cream. *Serves 8.*

2 cups cranberries

½ cup orange juice

1 cup granulated sugar

Pinch of salt

CRANBERRY COMPOTE

In a saucepan, bring all ingredients to a boil; reduce heat and simmer until berries are soft, about 20 minutes. Serve chilled. *Makes 2 cups.*

GINGER CHOCOLATE PEARS

THE COUNTRY SQUIRE, NARAMATA, BC

Truly a dessert that looks as if you spent hours preparing it, when, in fact, the recipe is very easy to create. Chef Patt Dyck of The Country Squire comments that the finest quality chocolate makes the most outstanding chocolate desserts. She suggests that if the pears are not super-sweet, you should add ¾ to 1 cup of sugar to the poaching liquid.

1 cup white wine

3 cups water

¾ to 1 cup sugar (optional, depending on sweetness of pears)

3 cinnamon sticks

12 whole cloves

6 allspice berries (or ¼ teaspoon ground allspice)

1 teaspoon ground nutmeg

6 to 8 small firm Bosc or Anjou pears

large bowl of acidulated water (cold water plus 1 tablespoon lemon juice)

Ginger Chocolate Sauce (recipe follows)

whipped cream

2 tablespoons candied ginger, finely diced

In a large deep saucepan over high heat, bring water, wine and spices to a boil; reduce heat and simmer 10 minutes. While poaching liquid is simmering, prepare pears.

Working with one pear at a time, slice the bottom end so that the pear can stand upright. Cradle the pear in your hand and with a small paring knife, hollow out the core, being careful not to cut into the sides of the pear. Peel pear, leaving the stem intact; immerse in acidulated water. Poach the pears, a few at a time, until tender. Stand pears to drain on a tray and cool completely.

To serve, place one chilled pear in the middle of a dessert plate and carefully coat the pear's surface with the hot Ginger Chocolate Sauce. Decorate the plate with freshly whipped cream and candied ginger. *Serves 6 to 8.*

6 ounces/175 grams semi-sweet baking chocolate

1 ounce/25 grams unsweetened baking chocolate

4 tablespoons butter

½ cup corn syrup

⅔ cup crème de cacao or coffee liqueur

1-inch/2.5-centimetre piece fresh ginger, peeled and cut in 3 pieces

½ cup cream (35% mf)

GINGER CHOCOLATE SAUCE

In the top of a double boiler over simmering water, melt chocolate, butter and corn syrup; whisk gently to combine. Remove sauce to a small, heavy-bottomed saucepan, add crème de cacao and ginger; simmer over low heat, stirring frequently, for 15 minutes. Add the cream and reheat. Remove the ginger before serving.

PRESERVES & CONDIMENTS

Some people feel that pickling and preserving has become a lost art. Indeed, the days when mother harvested the crops from her kitchen garden and preserved them for the cold winter months ahead is, for most of us, just a memory. We have, nevertheless, decided to include a few quick and easy recipes simply because there is no comparison between homemade and store-bought condiments.

We were fortunate to have our chefs share a few recipe gems — so why not try making your own flavoured vinegar or herb-infused oils?

Ah, let us not forget those prolific zucchini and green tomatoes — home gardeners can relate to the experience of being over run with these vegetables, so get out the preserving kettle and make Green Tomato Chow Chow or Sweet Zucchini Relish — your family will appreciate your efforts. And while you are in the preserving mood, why not tuck away a few jars of chutney. Try Curried Pineapple Chutney, the creation of the chefs at the Dundee Arms Hotel, or Mango Chutney, a condiment that complements curry dishes, chicken or pork, and is delightful served with cheese. Remember, jars of homemade oils, preserves or chutneys make wonderful host gifts!

◀ Sweet Zucchini Relish

GREEN TOMATO CHOW CHOW

Oh, what to do with that abundant supply of green tomatoes? You know, the ones that refuse to ripen after the first frost. Green Tomato Chow Chow makes a tasty accompaniment to fall and winter fare.

5 quarts/5 litres green tomatoes

6 large onions, thinly sliced

⅓ cup coarse pickling salt

4 cups white or cider vinegar

6 cups sugar

¼ cup pickling spice

Wash and thinly slice unpeeled tomatoes, place in a large glass bowl. Thinly slice onions and place in bowl with tomatoes. Sprinkle with pickling salt, stirring to cover vegetables evenly. Cover vegetables and let stand overnight.

Thoroughly rinse vegetables with cold running water and press out excess moisture. In a large saucepan, bring vinegar and sugar to a boil. Tie pickling spice in a cheesecloth bag and add to vinegar. Stir vegetables into vinegar and simmer until thickened and vegetables are soft, about 1½ hours. Ladle into hot sterilized jars and seal according to the manufacturer's directions. Store in a cool, dark cupboard up to one year. *Makes 12 cups.*

SWEET ZUCCHINI RELISH

To allow the flavours to blend, we suggest storing the relish two to three weeks before serving.

5 pounds/2.2 kilograms zucchini, seeded and chopped

1 cup sweet red pepper, chopped

½ cup sweet green pepper, chopped

3 cups onion, chopped

⅛ cup pickling salt

3 cups white vinegar

4½ cups granulated sugar

2 teaspoons dry mustard

1½ teaspoons celery seed

¾ teaspoon black pepper

¾ teaspoon turmeric

1 tablespoon cornstarch dissolved in 1 tablespoon cold water

In a large bowl, combine zucchini, peppers and onion; stir in pickling salt and let stand, covered, for two hours. Drain vegetables in a colander and rinse with cold running water. Squeeze out excess moisture.

In a large saucepan, combine vinegar, sugar, dry mustard, celery seed, black pepper and turmeric; bring to a boil. Add vegetables and simmer 30 minutes, stirring frequently. Stir cornstarch mixture into vegetables and continue to simmer 5 minutes until mixture is slightly thickened. Ladle relish into hot sterilized jars and seal according to the manufacturer's directions. Store in a cool dark place up to one year. *Makes 10 to 12 cups.*

MANGO CHUTNEY

A gift to us from East Indian cuisine, chutneys are condiments of simmered fruits, spices and vinegars. Chunky in consistency, this chutney is a delicious accompaniment to curries, pork and chicken entrees and also complements fresh fruit or cheese.

4 large mangoes, peeled and diced

2½ cups granulated sugar

1 cup brown sugar

1 cup cider vinegar

4 tablespoons fresh ginger, finely chopped

2 small jalapeno peppers, seeded and chopped

4 cloves garlic, finely chopped

1 teaspoon ground cardamom

1½ teaspoons whole cloves, tied in a cheesecloth bag

½ cup golden raisins

Combine mango and sugars in a large bowl, stirring until sugar dissolves. Cover and reserve overnight. Drain mango in a colander and reserve syrup.

In a heavy saucepan, combine vinegar, ginger, peppers, garlic, cardamom, dried cloves and reserved syrup. Bring to a boil over medium heat; reduce heat and simmer 30 minutes; remove cloves. Add mango and raisins; simmer 20 minutes. Ladle into hot sterilized jars and seal according to manufacturer's directions. *Makes 4 to 5 cups.*

SPIRITED CRANBERRY-ORANGE SAUCE

Choose either fresh or frozen cranberries for this recipe. If using frozen berries, you may need to extend the cooking time by a few minutes to allow the berries to "pop."

Juice and zest of 2 oranges
1 teaspoon fresh lemon juice
¾ cup granulated sugar
½ cup peeled apple, finely diced
3 cups cranberries
1 tablespoon brandy or cognac

In a heavy-based saucepan over medium heat, combine orange juice and zest, lemon juice, sugar and apple. Bring to a boil, stirring constantly, until sugar is dissolved; cook 4 minutes. Add cranberries and return to a boil; reduce heat and simmer, stirring frequently, until cranberries "pop," about 7 minutes. Remove from heat and stir in brandy. Refrigerate, covered, for up to 1 week. *Makes 2 cups.*

CURRIED PINEAPPLE CHUTNEY

THE DUNDEE ARMS, CHARLOTTETOWN, PEI

This creation of chef Patrick Young is served with Maple-Roasted Pork Loin, page 69, but is an ideal accompaniment to any pork or chicken dish. The quantities in this recipe may be doubled and stored in sterilized jars.

2 tablespoons vegetable oil

⅓ large red onion, chopped

½ large red bell pepper, chopped

2 tablespoons jalapeno pepper, seeds removed and minced

1 tablespoon curry powder

3 cups fresh pineapple cubes (or drained canned pineapple in its own juice)

½ cup orange juice

½ cup cider vinegar

½ cup brown sugar, packed

Salt and pepper to taste

Heat oil in a heavy saucepan over medium-low heat. Add red onions and red bell pepper and sauté, stirring frequently until onion begins to soften, about 8 minutes. Add jalapeno pepper and curry powder, stirring 2 minutes. Add pineapple, orange juice, cider vinegar and brown sugar; bring to a boil, reduce heat and simmer until mixture thickens, stirring often, about 1 hour. Season chutney with salt and pepper; cool completely, cover and refrigerate. *Makes 2½ cups.*

PLUM TOMATO CHUTNEY

INN AT SPRY POINT, SPRY POINT, PEI

Shirleen Peardon, the chef at Inn at Spry Point, serves this versatile tomato chutney with pork, fish, poultry and beef entrees. She is even known to spread it on crostini as an appetizer. It will keep refrigerated for 2 weeks.

½ cup red wine vinegar

¾ cup apple cider vinegar

⅔ cup sugar

¾ teaspoon salt

½ teaspoon pepper

½ teaspoon chili powder

1 pound/500 grams plum tomatoes, diced (preferably vine-ripened)

1 sweet red pepper, diced

5 green onions, sliced

In a medium saucepan over medium-high heat, bring vinegars, sugar, salt, pepper and chili powder to a boil. Add tomatoes, red pepper and green onions, bring back to boil; reduce heat and simmer, uncovered, stirring occasionally until thickened and reduced to 1½ cups, about 1 hour. Cool completely and store, covered, in the refrigerator. *Makes 1½ cups.*

HERB-INFUSED OIL

LITTLE INN OF BAYFIELD, BAYFIELD, ON

The innkeepers at Little Inn of Bayfield tell us that making infused oil is as simple as brewing tea. If the herbs in your garden appear gritty, wash them with a hose before picking and allow to air dry.

2¼ cups olive oil (or vegetable oil)

4 to 6 fresh large herb sprigs (rosemary, basil, oregano, thyme, tarragon, lemon balm, etc.)

In a heavy-based saucepan, heat oil to 200°F; add herbs, turn off burner and steep for 2 hours. Pour oil through a fine-meshed strainer, discarding herbs. To bottle, place a few sprigs of fresh herbs in a sterilized jar, add oil and seal with an airtight lid or stopper. Store in a cool dark place or refrigerate. If the oil solidifies when chilled, simply bring it to room temperature before use. Shelf life is a maximum of 6 months.

FLAVOURED VINEGAR

LITTLE INN OF BAYFIELD, BAYFIELD, ON

Infused vinegar, with its fresh, crisp flavour, elevates ordinary soup, vinaigrette and stew recipes into exciting creations. Make your own easily and economically in a matter of minutes. Pre-wash berries and herbs, but make sure they are completely dry before beginning the recipe.

Berry Vinegar:

1 cup fresh berries of choice (raspberry, blackberry, blueberry, etc.)

1¼ cups white wine vinegar

Herb Vinegar:

1 cup chopped herbs of choice (thyme, oregano, basil, rosemary, tarragon, dill, etc.)

1 clove garlic, crushed

4 cups vinegar of choice (white wine, red wine, cider, sherry, champagne, etc.)

Place berries or herbs in sterilized bottles with non-metallic lids or stoppers. Heat vinegar to boiling point in a non-aluminum saucepan. Pour vinegar over berries or herbs and cover with lids. Let stand at room temperature for 2 weeks.

Pour vinegar through a fine-mesh strainer lined with cheesecloth. Discard fruit or herbs; pour flavoured vinegar into sterilized bottles and seal with airtight lids or stoppers. Store in a cool dark place or refrigerate.

PICKLED BEETS

Beets are harvested in early autumn, and you should choose firm baby beets of uniform size. For optimum results, store the pickled beets sealed in jars in a cool, dark cupboard, and use within 6 months.

5 pounds/2.2 kilograms baby beets, washed

6 cups white vinegar

1½ cups water

3 cups sugar

1½ teaspoons salt

⅓ cup pickling spices

2 teaspoons mustard seeds

Simmer or steam beets until tender when pierced with a skewer, about 45 minutes. Drain and slip the skin from the beets with your fingers.

While the beets are cooking, combine vinegar, water, sugar and salt in a large preserving kettle; bring to a boil. Tie pickling spices and mustard seeds in a cheesecloth bag; add to vinegar, simmer 10 minutes and remove bag. Pack beets in hot sterilized jars, cover with vinegar mixture and seal, following manufacturer's directions. Store in a dark cupboard. *Makes 8 pints.*